# ROI for Nonprofits

## The New Key to Sustainability

## TOM RALSER

BICENTENNIAL
1807
WILEY
2007
BICENTENNIAL

John Wiley & Sons, Inc.

For general information on our other products and services, or technical support, please contact our Customer Care Department within the United States at 800-762-2974, outside the United States at 317-572-3993 or fax 317-572-4002.

Wiley also publishes its books in a variety of electronic formats. Some content that appears in print may not be available in electronic books.

For more information about Wiley products, visit our web site at http://www.wiley.com.

**Library of Congress Cataloging-in-Publication Data:**


ISBN: 978-0-470-50554-0


10   9   8   7   6   5   4

*To my family, whose love and support
allowed this book to happen.*

*And to those nonprofits who fight the good fight
and make the most of very little.*

# Table of Contents

# Foreword...Three Perspectives

Invoking economists from John Maynard Keynes to Adam Smith, and drawing on the sound principles of fundraising, *Return on Investment* hits hard at one of the biggest challenges we face in philanthropy: translating our impact into results that will be understood by our social investors. Recent studies of high-wealth individuals (U.S. Trust, Bank of America, 2007) once again reveal investors' concerns about how well their philanthropic gifts are used, and what their impact has been. These investors report they would give more if they had more confidence in the results. This book tackles those concerns and provides a clearly constructed method for analyzing "value" that should give nonprofits a new way to present their impact in both social and economic terms.

Several ideas emerge in this work. First, that all giving is investment. I agree: when I wrote *Beyond Fundraising* in 1997 and revised it in 2005, I gave it a subtitle of *New Strategies for Nonprofit Innovation and Investment*. While the word *investment* provoked some criticism and generated doubt in 1997 about the application of that word to our sector, by 2005 the belief in donor investment had become part of our philanthropic thinking. This book supports another related notion that I believe in, too: the "two-portfolio theory." We have a financial investment portfolio and a social investment portfolio. We take from one to enrich the other—what this book suggests is that there is a bigger win/win than I had imagined.

Second, that economic models can be applied successfully to measuring even the "soft" part of our sector. The book constructs intelligent models and offers strategies for implementing the ROI program that should provide the curious and the bold with an innovative and effective way to analyze, evaluate, and communicate with donor investors. In his preface, the author says the book isn't for everyone. But, for those whose organizations could benefit and are willing to give this a try, there are lots of tools to make it work.

Finally, the book adroitly weaves together the idea of "value" and "values"—realizing that the motivation for all philanthropy is shared *values* but shining new light on the idea that there has to be demonstrated *value* in the investment even if the shared values (and agreement with the mission and vision) are strong. By translating both the social and the economic impact, the return on investor values is multiplied.

ROI is a powerful concept, and one that can be tied strongly to twenty-first-century investor demands for accountability and transparency in the philanthropic sector. As wealth and philanthropy grow in the United States and globally, we need models like this to help us rethink the way we convey the full benefit of all that the nonprofit sector does to strengthen our communities.

Kay Sprinkel Grace
July 4, 2007

★ ★ ★

In 1984, I was asked by a small town hospital CEO to develop a *good* cardiac rehab program—which seemed interesting for a nurse with a cardiac care background. I soon learned however, that a good rehab program wasn't good enough, unless it generated revenue.

Just two years after the program was launched, the rehab schedule had a waiting list, an urban hospital became interested and wanted to establish a network for referrals, and perhaps most importantly, physicians gave the program high praise about its effectiveness based on their patients' improved health. But I'll never forget when that same CEO came to me to say I was to be laid off because the hospital was losing money on the program.

That was my first lesson in return on investment (ROI) and what I came to understand as social, clinical, and fiscal ROI. Who could have predicted that other powerful business lessons would emerge as a result of my work as a nurse in a small town and be followed by work at the state and national levels over the next 20 years?

Eventually I learned about cost centers, donor investments, outcome-based performance, and so on. And then in 2004, I met Tom Ralser, where during his presentation at a national conference I had an *Ah-ha* moment.

Here was a guy steeped in finance who understood the connections between the nonprofit sector and business development. He had a clear understanding of donors, nonprofits, sound business principles, and real-world applications. And while he didn't know health care, he certainly understood non-profits, both large and small. Before long we began working together on state and national conferences as well as among individual health care organizations. With lightning speed Tom learned about health care and was able to condense the confusion of health network development into easy-to-understand examples of what made sense. At the same time, he always presented the case for revenue generation, sustainability, and how both mission and funding were intrinsically linked. He introduced terminology, rationale, and common sense, anchored in some very sophisticated macro- and microeconomics. This book distills those lessons into a format that every nonprofit executive can benefit from reading.

By the way, I never did lose that cardiac rehab job—I just learned how to market the program to insurance companies and patients. Implementing the practices highlighted in this book can be a much easier way to learn.

Patricia J. Kota
CEO, Coastal Medical Access Project
May 2, 2007

★ ★ ★

Sustainability—the most sought after, yet often most illusive, goal of many not-for-profit organizations. In our work at the Georgia Health Policy Center, with hundreds of emerging and established organizations that seek to improve health and health access, help with sustainability is the number-one request.

Many of these organizations are community health initiatives—locally crafted responses to health care access problems—that have been steadfast in their efforts to connect uninsured and medically indigent people to health care services and health insurance. Typically, they unite community leaders, providers, and other key stakeholders, building on good-faith relationships to reduce uncompensated care and support the local safety net.

Despite their value to both individuals and the community as a whole, local initiatives are difficult to sustain. In a study of five cases, community leaders identified several organizational attributes as necessary for sustainability. Some of these include leaders, with a strong business sense, and partnerships that result in investment and data that help these initiatives demonstrate their value over time to a wide array of stakeholders. These organizational attributes are congruent with Tom's messages.

Tom Ralser has provided these organizations with a way to approach sustainability and practical tools that result in success. He has shown them the importance of being clear about organizational goals, placing a financial value on the achievement of the goals, and having conversations with partners that result in financial investment. The organizational leaders that have worked closely with Tom are more intentional, more confident about their organizational sustainability, and more successful at maneuvering the path to sustainability.

Karen Minyard, Ph.D.
Director, Georgia Health Policy Center
Andrew Young School of Policy Studies
Georgia State University

# Preface

They say you should write about what you know.

By training, education, and certification, I know about return on investment (ROI). I am probably as steeped in the ROI area as one can get. It started with my first finance class as an undergrad, where after receiving a surprisingly high grade, my interest in the subject was piqued. That prompted my entry into a masters program in finance that, upon completion, led to my earning the professional designation of Chartered Financial Analyst (CFA). I taught finance and investments to college seniors for seven years.

How does this relate to ROI and nonprofit sustainability?

In the early 1990s, I was living the good life in Grand Junction, Colorado. I was a 32-year-old tenured professor of finance at Mesa State College, a school where teaching still mattered. I had a great quality of life, and was living in the middle of the greatest mountain biking and whitewater area in the country. Then, two seemingly unrelated events coincided that brought about the confluence of a for-profit finance background and nonprofit funding.

The first had everything to do with being located in Grand Junction, Colorado. The resource-dependent Western town had gone through its share of boom and bust cycles. In the late 1970s and early 1980s, it was in the midst of another big boom. When the oil crisis hit in the mid-1970s, with oil peaking above the $40-a-barrel mark, the solution according to the big oil companies and the federal government was oil shale. Oil shale is underground rock full of keragen, a waxy petroleum, and much of Western Colorado sits on top of it. This part of the country has been referred to as "the next Saudi Arabia," and one basin alone has been estimated to contain 300 billion barrels of recoverable petroleum, equal to 48 percent of Middle Eastern reserves [Clifford].

The challenge was not to drill a hole and hope to find oil, but to get the oil out of the rock in a cost-effective manner. With oil predicted to hit $70 a barrel someday (hard to believe, isn't it?), suddenly many options were approaching profitability. Plans were made that would excavate the equivalent of the Panama Canal every month [Williamson].

A little company named Exxon, fat with federal contracts, invaded the Grand Junction area and set up shop. Actually, they built a town, not unlike the company towns of the Old West. The town was designed to provide infrastructure for the large number of people needed to make the oil shale project work. In total, they invested an estimated $5 billion in what was called the Colony Project.

As happens in any localized economic boom cycle, prices on everything from food to housing went up. There was a new influx of people, with big paychecks to spend. The housing market could not keep up. The story was told more than once of how people would pay $400 a month (that's in 1982 dollars) to rent covered porches to use them as a home until something better came along.

As suddenly as it began, it stopped. The boom turned to bust. On a day known locally as Black Sunday, May 2, 1982, Exxon pulled the plug on the project. The decision would bring an end to thousands of jobs on that project alone, not to mention the ripple effects that would follow. Most who moved in for the work could not move out fast enough. Many tried to stay, because Grand Junction is such a great place to live, but there were only so many opportunities.

The laws of economics took over. Housing prices fell. Unemployment rose. With fewer dollars circulating in the local economy, businesses closed their doors. One year later, foreclosures in Grand Junction and Mesa County quadrupled their 1980 numbers, and bankruptcies doubled [Williamson]. The townspeople decided they had to do something.

They formed a nonprofit called the Mesa County Economic Development Council (MCEDC). Their objective was to recruit companies and bring in jobs. They needed money to operate, so they held a fundraising campaign, and raised approximately $1.3 million to be spent over four years. After four years, they raised more money to be spent over the next four years.

As the end of this second four-year cycle drew near, several community leaders approached me to become the founding director of the Western Colorado Bureau of Economic and Business Research. Various public sector entities, such as the City of Grand Junction, the school district, and Mesa County, wanted the capacity for economic modeling and reporting to exist locally. Since this capacity existed at most colleges and universities, Mesa State was eager to do its share and provided the physical space and a faculty member to direct it. That faculty member was yours truly.

At the end of their second four-year funding period, MCEDC had to decide if there would be a third. The economy was now much better. People were happier. The cost of raising that money, though, was high. The fundraiser they had used previously certainly wanted them to do it again. It became a standoff, with the agreement that the Western Colorado Bureau of Business and Economic Research would determine if the money spent by MCEDC was worth it; did it provide an acceptable ROI?

We did our analysis, having to make the econometric models from scratch, since economics at the local level is a bit messy for the tastes of most academics and professional economists. Data at the local level is often spotty and subject to many externalities, but we muddled through and presented our findings at a breakfast for all the important people in town. The findings were very good; the amount spent by MCEDC over eight years, compared to the impact it had on the economy, was 17 to 1.

After the presentation, a well-dressed man approached me. I knew he was not local, since he was too nicely dressed and I knew almost everyone in town. He said he was MCEDC's fundraiser, and that my presentation had just sealed the deal on his being hired for a third round of fundraising. That was my introduction to the marriage of for-profit techniques applied to nonprofit funding. It was 1993.

The second event had everything to do with running my very own nonprofit. As head of the Western Colorado Bureau of Economic and Business Research, I also needed to pay attention to the finances of my own organization. While we did not engage in fundraising per se, the organization needed to keep its own funders happy, which in turn allowed the financial support to continue. I told them what research we were providing, why it was valuable, and why it was important to the community to keep the checks coming.

Because of the success with the MCEDC process, my services became known to the fundraising community, and over the next several years I started working with fundraisers on a national basis. They saw something I initially did not: My corporate finance and investment analysis background dovetailed very nicely with the nonprofit world, especially fundraising. What was originally done because I did not know any better became valued by professional fundraisers in getting them hired and making their jobs easier.

What has become a cornerstone of our work today was not obvious at first; the process used by the for-profit world of investment banking was strikingly similar to the process that worked extremely well for nonprofit fundraising:

1.  Make a compelling case for investment.
2.  Get investors to commit.
3.  Produce something they value.

In 1994, I left the academic world to grow this niche business. The process that was originally used by other fundraisers worked so well that it is now used in our own fundraising business. The process has moved beyond economic development groups to many categories of nonprofits: arts and culture, health services, education, sports and recreation, environmental, urban redevelopment, and community services. We have worked in 48 states, from local to national efforts. I say this not as a promotion for our business, but to let the reader know that the concepts in this book are not theories, but proven, field-tested techniques. They have been used in rural counties as small as 12,000 people, and in major metropolitan areas such as Seattle, Orlando, and Atlanta.

Many who are versed in the classic world of fundraising (and there are many) will find reasons to disagree with some of the material presented in the following pages. They have a huge investment in the status quo, and want to protect it. They want people to believe that raising money for nonprofits is a complicated, secret, and mystical experience, one that cannot possibly be done independently. To be sure, it is hard work, but the concept of hard work is familiar to those who choose to work in the nonprofit business.

This book will benefit the smaller nonprofits most, those with annual budgets under $10 million. This group shares a common set of problems that larger, name-brand nonprofits do not: little name recognition, boards with limited financial capacity, and missions that carry little status. These organizations are struggling every day to fulfill their mission and remain financially sustainable. They often look with envy or amazement at the larger, name-brand nonprofits that raise hundreds of millions of dollars each year.

This book provides an overview of the need to focus on delivering value, and specific methods on how to demonstrate it. If even an isolated concept or a single idea rises to the surface of the reader's consciousness, this book has accomplished something. If even one nonprofit that produces valuable outcomes can use the information to help it obtain funding to continue its work, this book will have succeeded.

## ▨ REFERENCES

Clifford, Hal. "Colorado Oil Shale Gets a Second Look," *High Country News*, March 4, 2002, www.hcn.org/servlets/hcn.PrintableArticle?article_id=11056.

Williamson, Richard. "Oil Shale Collapse Preserved Scenic Vistas," *Denver Rocky Mountain News*, October 5, 1999. Accessed October 24, 2006, http://www.denver-rmn.com/millennium/1005mile.shtml.

# Introduction

Having the audacity to say that something is a "key" to anything is bold. Stating it in a way that challenges the status quo may be a bad business decision. Knowing that it is likely to upset many people, yet still going through with it, may be pure stupidity.

The concepts in this book are not theories.
They are not academic suppositions that are untested in the real world.
They are not far-left or far-right observations designed to initiate discussion.
The concepts in this book do not replace solid fundraising.
They accentuate it. They enhance it. They augment it.

What are presented are observations of a fundamental shift that has occurred over the last 15 years in the nonprofit world, and how nonprofits can take advantage of it. What is this shift? The shift to value being demanded by those who invest in nonprofits. And when that value is delivered, the investment follows.

## WHO MIGHT BENEFIT FROM READING THIS BOOK

*Nonprofits* that have found that traditional methods for raising money are not producing the results they expected. The traditional methods of volunteer-driven campaigns that rely more on cheerleading and twisting the arms of friends than on solid reasons for investment still abound (see *Five Classic Misconceptions* in Chapter 3). This book represents a major change in how to capitalize on the motivations of those who are likely to invest in your organization.

*Nonprofits that do good work and need to demonstrate it.* Very few nonprofits have a limitless funding source. In the era of tight money and increasing numbers looking for it, this demonstration of value becomes even more critical.

*Investors in nonprofits who are looking for reasons to continue, or even increase, their investment in a nonprofit.* The corporate world, probably more than any other group, is looking to make sure their dollars are being used effectively. Demonstrating ROI and the value of an organization's efforts is extremely useful in this regard.

*Foundations looking to implement an ROI-based framework.* Many foundations are looking to make their grant process as socially impacting as possible. Foundations can conduct an apples-to-apples comparison between grant requests by designing a standardized framework into their application process to demonstrate ROI, rather than just saying, "Explain the outcome expected from your proposed effort."

*Nonprofits with small staffs and no dedicated development person.* Hiring outside counsel to help with raising money is expensive. The farther along your organization is in the evolution of providing value to investors, the less time outside counsel will need to spend on developing your case statement, which allows more time to be spent on actually presenting your case.

*Nonprofits that have never embarked on a capital campaign.* The concepts presented can be integrated into all newsletters, communications, and meetings/events. This will set the stage for enhanced credibility should a campaign be launched in the future.

*Fundraisers who are looking to build a stronger case for support.* At any given point in time, our ROI material is in use in anywhere from 15 to 20 campaigns across the country. Professional fundraisers have been using it for over 12 years now, and continue to demand it for high-level asks.

*Nonprofits caught in the downward spiral of grant funding.* Total dependence on grants for funding is risky, and likely to disappear at some point. Many grants are now for a limited number of years, so the search for new grants is never-ending. Adding private investors to the funding portfolio reduces risk and improves the chances of long-term, sustainable funding.

***Board members*** *looking for reasons to finally launch a campaign.* They may have felt the process was too complicated, or cost too much, or that the organization just didn't have the right to ask for money. Developing an ROI-based program of work that is focused on value will make that step easier to finally take.

## WHO MIGHT DISAGREE WITH THIS BOOK

***Large universities, big hospitals, and established arts and culture organizations*** that have alumni, customers, and members who already give them money. It would not be smart to rock the boat. These classic examples of traditional ivy-covered institutions have been raising money for years. Lots of money. They know how to capitalize on their constituents' motivations:

- Improving the library of your alma mater will make that particular institution a better school, which will reflect positively on you throughout you career.
- Your local hospital needs to have a top-rate emergency room, since you may find yourself needing care there someday.
- The local museum must build that new wing in order to accept that new collection, which raises the culture quotient of the community in which you live and provides a higher quality of life.

***Traditional fundraising houses*** that have been around almost as long as nonprofits themselves. They often specialize in certain geographic areas, carefully maintaining large databases of names of those who give what to whom, and sitting on as many nonprofit boards as possible to get the first whiff of potential new business. They, like the nonprofit organizations mentioned previously, do not want a new concept to confuse their established list of donors. They would then have to change their sales pitch, which might be bad for business.

***Those who believe that "people give to people, not causes."*** This party line of volunteer-driven fundraising is true, but is only part of the equation. People also give to causes. When the right people, cause, *and* value are combined, magic can happen. This issue is discussed in Chapter 3.

Whether the readers find themselves in one of the preceding categories or not, this book will provide a basis for discussion that will surely continue. Approval from those in the industry is not the goal; the goal is to help nonprofits that provide value become more financially sustainable organizations.

This book is divided into two main sections. Chapters 1 through 6 establish the benefits and motivations for the investment-driven approach. This is the "Why" portion of the book. Chapters 7 through 10 demonstrate the range in which ROI can be put to use and comprise the "How?" portion of the book.

# About the Author

Tom Ralser, CFA, has worked with nonprofits in 48 states on over 350 funding projects. His work has ranged from national corporate sponsorships to statewide economic development campaigns to local human services efforts. Fundraisers have described his work as the "silver bullet" that justifies larger investments, and nonprofits use his planning techniques to ensure long-term sustainability.

He was first pulled away from his tenured position as a professor of finance in 1992, when he was asked by a local nonprofit to demonstrate how their work had impacted their community. This led to his forming Capital Strategists Group, a fundraising and planning company dedicated to making nonprofits sustainable by moving them from a charity mindset to one of investment. ROImetrix, his more quantitatively oriented company, works not only with traditional nonprofits on demonstrating ROI, but with corporations, foundations, and individuals to confirm that the nonprofits in which they invest are truly delivering outcomes with value.

# PART ONE

# Why ROI?

# CHAPTER 1

# Demystifying the Status Quo

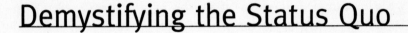

**JOHN MAYNARD KEYNES** *The difficulty lies, not in the new ideas, but in escaping the old ones, which ramify, for those brought up as most of us have been, into every corner of our minds.*

Nonprofits are not that different from for-profits. This statement alone causes heated discussion and may lead many to dismiss the concepts in this book. The management skills needed may be different. The "mission" is different. The single concept that is not different is that both nonprofits and for-profits must *provide value to investors*. If a for-profit organization does not do this, the market puts it out of business. If a nonprofit does not do this, the market does not fund it.

## THEY'RE BIG AND IN BUSINESS

Nonprofits are big business, with special emphasis on the words *big* and *business*. Americans gave over $260 *billion* to nonprofits in 2005, according to *Giving USA*, the annual yearbook on philanthropy. Who gave what?

| *Who* | *How Much* | *Percent* |
| --- | --- | --- |
| Individuals | $199 billion | 76.5 |
| Foundations | $30 billion | 11.5 |
| Bequests | $17 billion | 6.7 |
| Corporations | $13 billion | 5.3 |

What does this say? Americans are generous? Yes. Individuals give far more than anyone else? Yes. Corporations, by comparison, are rather stingy? Yes. But these numbers alone do not tell the whole story.

*Giving USA* is also astute enough to track where the money goes, by type of organization. The religion category, comprised of churches and other religious organizations, happens to attract the largest share at over $93 billion, almost 36 percent of all contributions. Subtracting the $93 billion from the $260 billion leaves $167 billion for the rest of the nonprofits in this country.

According to the National Center for Charitable Statistics, in 2004 there were approximately 1.8 million nonprofit organizations registered with the Internal Revenue Service (IRS) in this country:

850,000 public charities

104,000 private foundations

464,000 miscellaneous types

377,000 churches/congregations

Now bring in some facts from different sources. The January 2006 Harris Interactive DonorPulse survey reported that about half of those who gave to charitable organizations in 2005 gave less than $500. Only 6 percent said they gave $5,000 or more. They also report that in 2005, the largest percentage of donors, approximately 50 percent, gave to churches and religious organizations. In 2004, the National Center for Charitable Statistics also reports that public charities reported nearly $1.1 trillion in total revenues, with 23 percent coming from contributions, gifts, and grants; 71 percent coming from program revenues (which include government contracts and fees); and 6 percent from other sources (including dues, special events income, rents, and products sold).

Simple arithmetic lets us paint a picture of an "average" public charity. If one divides the 850,000 public charities into the $1.1 trillion in total revenues, it yields an average annual budget of $1.29 million. Looking at it another way, dividing the sum of 850,000 public charities, 104,000 private foundations, and 464,000 miscellaneous organizations into the $167 billion given to nonreligious organizations yields about $118,000 per year from private sources for each organization.

Here is the picture that emerges of the nonreligious nonprofit landscape:

- Many organizations are competing for dollars.
- Relatively small amounts of total funding come from private sources.
- Private contributions are usually in small amounts.
- There is a heavy dependence on government funding.

We go from hundreds of billions of dollars in aggregate to an average of $118,000 per organization from private sources. Many nonprofits have come to rely on getting the majority of their funding from the government. What does come from the private sector is reminiscent of a tin cup and begging, rather than being funded because of the good work being done. This vision seems to reinforce the negative connotations of *charity*, in every sense of the word. One has to wonder if this is the way in which America wants its nonprofits to operate.

Not only are nonprofits big business, but the thousands of companies that make their collective living by selling them things are big business, too, especially those involved in helping them raise money. Let's just look at some of the household names everyone knows, the brand-name nonprofits: the American Cancer Society, the Red Cross, and the Salvation Army.

According to the *Chronicle of Philanthropy*, which annually publishes *The Philanthropy 400*, a listing of the largest charities based on their "ability to attract private support," all of these nonprofits are in the top five in terms of amounts raised in the United States in 2005. The American Cancer Society raised over $929 million, the Red Cross over $1.27 billion, and the Salvation Army over $3.59 billion. The amounts spent on fundraising, rounded down to the nearest million, were $188 million, $118 million, and $137 million, respectively. Just these three nonprofits alone spent over $443 million on fundraising in just one year.

Just how this money was spent reads just like a for-profit business. Marketing certainly makes up a large part of it. So does technology, salaries, and outside consulting services.

The fact that three nonprofits spent $443 million to raise approximately $5.8 billion raises several questions. Is this good? From whose perspective? More importantly, did it provide an acceptable return on investment (ROI)?

To answer the first and second questions simultaneously, yes, it is good from society's perspective. These three nonprofits appear to be very good at what they do in terms of the societal good they provide. From a nonprofit's cost point of view, the answer is also yes. The ratio of fundraising expenses to private support dollars was 20.3 percent for the American Cancer Society, 9.3 percent for the Red Cross, and 3.8 percent for the Salvation Army. Collectively, the cost of raising funds was around 8.3 percent.

Can most nonprofits compare themselves to these three examples, or even the Philanthropy 400? Certainly not, since a given nonprofit had to raise over $37.7 million in 2005 just to break into the Philanthropy 400. Since the average annual budget for a public charity is somewhere in the neighborhood of $1.3 million, most have a long way to go.

The question of providing an acceptable level of ROI is more difficult to answer. Anecdotally, it must have provided an acceptable level of ROI to the organizations, since they continue to spend large amounts of money on fundraising year after year. Theoretically, a numerator of funds received divided by a denominator of the cost to raise the funds produces an ROI of $5.8 billion divided by $443 million, or 13 times. Most of us would be hard pressed to come up with a return that paid 13 times our investment in one year. But again, most nonprofits do not have the luxury of spending relatively large amounts of money on fundraising, even if it does generate 13 dollars for every one spent.

The preceding paragraph surfaces a central issue when discussing ROI and nonprofits: Most of the time, the discussion revolves around the issue of *fundraising effectiveness*, and that is not the point. It is not about how much was spent to raise how much more, at least from an outside investor's perspective. Prospective investors in a nonprofit want to know "What was accomplished with my money?" not "How much was spent on getting my money?" (within certain limits, of course). They want to know that the cause they believe in is being addressed: whether a positive effort is being enhanced, or a negative circumstance is being eliminated.

## FACTS ARE FACTS

This book is based on both qualitative and quantitative foundations. It is said that morality describes how things should work, and economics describes how things actually work. The strong economic flavor will become apparent very quickly.

Formal logic is a good place to introduce the premise of what follows. *Modus ponens* is a basic form of logic, which states that

If P, then Q.

P.

Therefore, Q.

Applying this logic to the current situation of funding for nonprofits, we get the following argument:

1. If a nonprofit demonstrates results, then Individuals, Corporations, and Foundations will fund it.

2. A nonprofit has demonstrated results.

3. Therefore, Individuals, Corporations, and Foundations will fund it.

Obviously, funding a nonprofit is not this easy, but the logic still holds. Consider these facts:

Fact 1.   Individuals, Corporations, and Foundations will fund non-profits.

Fact 2.   Individuals, Corporations, and Foundations invest in results.

Fact 3.   There is increasing competition for dollars.

Conclusion:   The nonprofit that demonstrates results is more likely to be funded.

In other words, the charity model that many nonprofits have adopted will become less and less effective in the future as competition for dollars becomes more intense. Most nonprofits intuitively understand this, but many are still reluctant to embrace the concept of nonprofit investment. Hopefully, this book will help eliminate that reluctance.

## THEY'RE EVERYWHERE

Chances are you have been directly touched by a nonprofit. You also might not have realized it. Perhaps you have been a member, worked directly for the organization, served on a committee or board, attended an event, or bought what they are selling.

If any of these apply, you are living proof of my assertion:

You have gone to church.

You have attended college.

You volunteer your time.

You donate used clothes.

You bought popcorn from the little league.

You got your car washed in the fast-food parking lot.

You sent in your alumni dues.

You renewed your membership to Ducks Unlimited, the Sierra Club, or the local Corvette Club.

You bought something at a bake sale.

You attended the symphony.

You went to the museum.

You served food at the soup kitchen.

You ate food at the soup kitchen.

You ran in a 5k race.

You wear a yellow latex band on your wrist.

You have paid admission to a college basketball game.

You bought a beer at the local arts festival.

The list goes on and on.

Why does this matter? People often have the misconception that a nonprofit is a completely different species of animal than the usual for-profit business, and not something familiar to them. Although some differences certainly do exist, this book demonstrates that while nonprofits may be a different animal, they are in the same species, and are more like first cousins. This is especially true when examining the aspect of sustainable funding; both for-profits and nonprofits must address it to effectively carry out their missions.

This book focuses on the one aspect of nonprofits that has not changed in decades: Nonprofits need to raise money. The fact that nonprofits need to raise money is not in question; however, the best way to do it is. The foundation for this book, and the key point borrowed from the for-profit world that is not different, is that both nonprofits and for-profits must do one thing to be successful:

*Provide value to investors.*

## Investors and Value

The two pivotal words in the statement "provide value to investors" are *investors* and *value*. Let's first talk about nonprofit investors. Yes, nonprofits have investors. People, foundations, and corporations give nonprofits money in return for something. That is what an investor does. Not an investor as in an equity position, complete with shares of stock and legal claims on assets, but an investor in that they expect something in return for their money. The challenge is in identifying what the investors expect and then giving it to them.

All of the following are examples of nonprofit investors, and they come in many shapes and sizes:

- The wealthy widow who makes a large gift to the hospital where her husband died to help fund the new cancer wing
- The couple who retires to a new community and gives to the community college where they take that long-awaited scuba diving class
- The local small-business person who helps build the new soccer field
- The foundation that helps fund the startup of a community center for teenage mothers so they can continue their education
- The large corporation that invests in regional economic development efforts to make the area more economically attractive
- The entrepreneur who endows a chair at his alma mater
- The homeowner in the neighborhood who buys door-to-door popcorn
- The average person shopping at Christmas time who drops some change in the red bucket outside the department store

Now for that other interesting word in the statement "provide value to investors": *value*. Many books have been written on values (plural) and their relationships to nonprofits. One of the very best is Kay Sprinkel Grace's *Beyond Fundraising*. It contains a great discussion on values-based mission statements, and differentiates between philanthropy, development, and fundraising. The very first sentence of the very first chapter says it all, "Philanthropic behavior is motivated by values."

Her point cannot be debated; people will not fund (or donate time, energy, or knowledge to) those organizations whose values they do not share. When the values of the investor (or donor if you must) align with the nonprofit organization, both parties benefit. As she states:

> At the most altruistic, this motivation draws people into selfless involvement with organizations that are advancing and strengthening basic community and individual values. At the other end of the continuum, there will be those whose initial motivation is the WIIFM (What's in it for me?).

This book deals with those precisely at that other end of the continuum, the "What's in it for me?" camp, and here's why. Many of the nonprofits we have dealt with over the last dozen or so years do not have the luxury of an internal development office. They cannot dedicate staff to development, or fundraising (if that word must be used). They typically have short timelines for funding (read *need money sooner rather than later*), and do not have the budget to devote to ad campaigns or lots of glossy collateral material. In other words, the distance between Point A (a potential funder) and Point B (a check arriving in the mail) has to be short. We have found, over and over again, that the shortest distance between these two points, in the fastest time possible, is the credible demonstration that the outcomes effectuated by the nonprofit are valuable. If the right value, in the true economic sense, is conveyed to potential funders, they become investors.

## Value and Values

Part of the confusion may have to do with the difference between the words *value* and *values*. In the *Beyond Fundraising* context, values are the principles, ideals, ethics, and morals of a given society. Value, in the "What's in it for me" camp, is the getting of something in return proximate to what is given. When one spends $20 on a hamburger, it had better be a good hamburger. When one gives $100,000 to a nonprofit, it had better deliver value *and* be consistent with one's values.

These two points are pivotal for the investment-driven model, discussed in detail later, to work for nonprofits:

1. The nonprofit must provide outcomes that have *value*, that is, outcomes that are desired.

2. The outcomes must be consistent with the *values* of the investor.

In defense of the WIIFM folks, they have their altruistic facets also. They are not looking for personal gain per se, but for community or societal gain. By virtue of being members of that community or society, however, they are gaining personally as well.

## They Are Different

There are, of course, differences between nonprofits and for-profits. While the philosophical differences could be, and probably will be, argued for years, these three are facts:

### 1. Their Economic Impact (Officially) Is Lower

All economic activity has an impact, and there is quite an industry dependent on demonstrating that impact. One of the common ways to determine that impact is with the use of input-output multipliers. Multipliers measure the so-called ripple effect, which is an analogy to the concentric ripples that form in the water when a stone is tossed into it. The tossed stone produces successive ripples that get larger and larger until they dissipate into the original surface of the water. An initial economic action causes another economic action to occur, with each action cumulatively adding to the impact of those that come before it.

To illustrate this difference in impact, let's compare several sets of multipliers across industries in a given geographic area. Using the Seattle area RIMS multipliers as an example, Exhibit 1.1 provides the direct earnings and

**EXHIBIT 1.1    DIRECT EFFECT INDUSTRY MULTIPLIERS: GENERAL INDUSTRY**

|  | Earnings Multiplier | Employment Multiplier |
| --- | --- | --- |
| Water transportation | 4.3945 | 6.2978 |
| Retail trade | 1.9609 | 1.6900 |
| Telecommunications | 2.2479 | 3.0535 |
| Construction | 1.9943 | 2.2754 |
| Aircraft manufacturing | 2.4886 | 4.4270 |
| Paper and paperboard mills | 2.6748 | 4.1881 |
| Average | 2.6268 | 3.6553 |

**EXHIBIT 1.2    DIRECT EFFECT INDUSTRY MULTIPLIERS: SOCIAL SERVICE SECTORS**

|  | Earnings Multiplier | Employment Multiplier |
|---|---|---|
| Social assistance | 1.7875 | 1.4326 |
| Performing arts companies | 1.8049 | 1.2161 |
| Museums, historical sites, zoos, and parks | 2.0254 | 2.0708 |
| Religious organizations | 1.5540 | 1.4598 |
| Grantmaking, giving, and social advocacy | 2.1683 | 2.2119 |
| Civic, social, and professional organizations | 1.9520 | 1.6470 |
| Average | 1.8820 | 1.6730 |

employment effect multipliers for six basic industry sectors that are a good representation of the Seattle economy.

Exhibit 1.2 provides the same multipliers for six sectors that are traditionally populated with nonprofits.

For every job in the private sector, using the average of the six industries, an additional 2.66 jobs are created within the geographic area. Each dollar paid in earnings by this same group begets an additional $1.63 in earnings in the area. Contrasting these results with the average of the nonprofit sample yields only .68 additional jobs and $.88 in additional earnings.

Why is this? The manufacturing sector, for example, typically takes a raw material, performs a process that adds value, and sells the product at a higher price. The retail sector buys products, inventories them, and resells them at a higher price. The nonprofit sector, however, does not purchase raw material, or resell a product after it is processed. It doesn't require a lot of expensive equipment or large blocks of real estate. Their value is typically more intangible and labor intensive, and fewer economic events occur from the input to the output stage; therefore, their multiplier is smaller and their impact is lower.

Not only does classical economic impact analysis of nonprofits (using techniques such as input–output tables) produce a lower value, but what these methods fail to measure is the very core of what nonprofits often address, such as the value of disease prevention, reducing negative social consequences, and lowering opportunity costs. In other words, while classical input–output analysis is valuable, it is based on a more industrial economy, not a service economy, which is where nonprofits generally find themselves.

## 2. They Pay Less

Salaries are generally lower in nonprofit organizations than in the for-profit world, but how much they vary depends on the source. Rather than use data supplied by the various philanthropic and nonprofit trade groups, which could be viewed as biased, or combing through IRS Form 990s, which have their own limitations for analysis purposes, this analysis will use government-supplied information. This comparison uses May 2005 National Industry-Specific Occupational Employment and Wage Estimates information from the Bureau of Labor Statistics (BLS), the most recent information available across all categories as of this publication.

The BLS created the North American Industry Classification System (NAICS) system to replace the outdated Standard Industrial Code (SIC) to more accurately reflect the changing economy, and provides information collected from employers who, by law, must report accurate information. This system is more useful than information collected, for instance, from the surveys of individuals about their employment status, the results of which are subject to the understanding or honesty of the person who answers the survey.

The major sectors presented in Exhibit 1.3 list the average annual wage of all occupations within the sector, and the average annual wage of only those considered to be in a management position.

The difficulty in determining how nonprofit compensation differs from for-profit compensation stems from the classification system itself; there is no nonprofit category. Since the information is not sorted by nonprofit versus for-profit, but rather by industry classification, one cannot reach a conclusion about nonprofit compensation. Digging deeper, though, and examining those specific six-digit industry classifications in which most

| EXHIBIT 1.3 | AVERAGE ANNUAL WAGE BY MAJOR INDUSTRY SECTOR | | |
|---|---|---|---|
| **Major Category** | | **All Occupations** | **Management Positions** |
| Professional, scientific, and technical services | | $58,560 | $113,090 |
| Retail | | $26,360 | $ 81,200 |
| Manufacturing | | $39,240 | $ 99,900 |
| Health care and social assistance | | $39,400 | $ 71,410 |

EXHIBIT 1.4    **AVERAGE ANNUAL WAGE BY SIX-DIGIT CLASSIFICATION**

| Major Category | All Occupations | Management Positions |
|---|---|---|
| Civic and social organizations (NAICS 813400) | $24,490 | $61,950 |
| Social assistance (NAICS 624000) | $25,760 | $53,970 |
| Individual and family services (NAICS 624100) | $28,170 | $59,010 |
| Services for the elderly and persons with disabilities (NAICS 624120) | $23,860 | $58,510 |
| Community food and housing, and emergency and other relief services (NAICS 624200) | $30,670 | $57,270 |
| Performing arts companies (NAICS 711100) | $41,440 | $77,400 |
| Museums, historical sites, and similar institutions (NAICS 712000) | $31,360 | $82,150 |
| Social advocacy organizations (NAICS 813300) | $35,330 | $69,300 |

nonprofits find themselves, reveals a more accurate picture as presented in Exhibit 1.4.

While it is true that nonprofits generally pay less than for-profit enterprises or government positions, new information from the *BLS Quarterly Census of Employment and Wages* reveals some interesting new insights. As reported in the September 2005 *BLS Monthly Labor Review,* for-profit firms paid wages that averaged 11 percent higher than nonprofits in 2002. However, in industries where both nonprofits and for-profits are involved, nonprofit wages actually equal or exceed those of for-profits in some areas.

This somewhat surprising picture emerges when industry aggregations are replaced with specific IRS designations regarding nonprofit or for-profit, and combined with detailed industry information. When this is done, hospitals and nursing homes are at approximately the same wage levels, their IRS designation notwithstanding. In the areas of education, social services, residential care, and day care, "nonprofit wages actually exceed the for-profit wages of their counterparts, often by a substantial margin."

The gist of this article, and its relevance to our discussion here, is nicely summarized by one sentence:

> What this suggests is that the apparent disadvantage of nonprofit wages is more an industry phenomenon, reflecting the fields in which nonprofits are active, than it is a sector phenomenon, reflecting the human resource policies of nonprofit agencies.

And that is precisely the point. Where nonprofits must compete with for-profits, they must pay industry-standard wages to stay competitive in the marketplace. It is in those areas where for-profits fear to tread, where there is a need but nobody willing to fill it because they cannot make a profit, that nonprofits step in to help. It is these nonprofits, when aggregated with the few that pay industry-standard wages, that lower the average nonprofit sector wage level.

## 3. They Play by a Different Set of Rules

Nonprofits, as most would describe them, are usually considered 501 (c) (3) organizations, the largest category of tax-exempt organizations classified by the IRS. Of the 20+ possible categories, only 7 qualify to receive tax-deductible contributions. Nonprofits need a ruling from the IRS in order to operate as a nonprofit that is exempt from income tax and for donors to be able to deduct contributions. This ruling is the one additional hoop they must jump through. That is it. They do not need a certain level of capitalization. They do not need to identify their strategic strengths. They just need to apply and meet three generalized tests.

The textbook *Financial and Strategic Management for Nonprofit Organizations* does a good job of describing these three tests.

**The Organizational Test**  This test states that the nonprofit must be organized for a lawful purpose in the one of following eight areas:

1. Educational
2. Religious
3. Charitable
4. Scientific
5. Literary
6. Testing for public safety
7. Fostering certain national or international amateur sports competitions
8. Preventing cruelty to children or animals

Since it would be relatively easy to conduct the preceding with a motive for making money, the IRS also requires that the motive not be one of advancing the private welfare of individuals, or what is known as the profit motive to most people. The motive must be one of charity; that is, the beneficiaries must be the community or the public in general. Specifically, the IRS states the following:

> (ii) An organization is not organized or operated exclusively for one or more of the purposes specified in subdivision (i) of this subparagraph unless it serves a public rather than private interest. Thus, to meet the requirement of this subdivision, it is necessary for an organization to establish that it is not organized or operated for the benefit of private interests such as designated individuals, the founder or his or her family, shareholders of the organization, or persons controlled, directly or indirectly, by such private interests.
>
> —[Treasury Regulations, Section 1.50 (c) (3) − 1, (d) (1) (ii), 1980]

The IRS further requires that specific purposes be identified, describing in more detail what the nonprofit does and in what general areas it operates.

**The Political Test**    Organizations desiring 501 (c) (3) status must also state in their organizing document that they will not participate in any political campaign on behalf of a candidate or make expenditures for political purposes. Other 501 designations may do this, but not 501 (c) (3) organizations.

**The Asset Test**    The nonprofit must also state in its charter that it prohibits the distribution of assets or income to individuals except as fair compensation for services rendered. It must also state that it will not be used for the personal gain or benefit of the founders, employees, supporters, relatives, or associates.

If these three tests are met, and all the accompanying paperwork is in good order, the nonprofit will likely become a tax-exempt, 501 (c) (3) organization. Then the challenges really begin.

## FINAL THOUGHTS

Nonprofits are different from for-profits, and can be very different from each other. Their varying characteristics, from budgets ranging in the billions to the thousands, and programs ranging from arts and culture to human services, do not make for a one-size-fits-all process of demonstrating return on investment. Add to this the changing philanthropic environment discussed in the next chapter, and one can see that motivations, outcomes, and methodologies all merit further exploration.

## ■ REFERENCES

Salamon, Lester M. and S. Wojciech Sokolowski. "Nonprofit Organizations: New Insights from QCEW Data." *BLS Monthly Labor Review* (September 2005, p. 24).

May 2005 National Industry-Specific Occupational Employment and Wage Estimates. May 2005 OES. Accessed December 31, 2006, http://www.bls.gov/oes/current/oessrci.htm.

Bryce, Herrington J. *Financial and Strategic Management for Nonprofit Organizations: A Comprehensive Reference to Legal, Financial, Management, and Operations Rules and Guidelines for Nonprofits, Third Ed.* (San Francisco: Jossey-Bass, 2000).

Grace, Kay Sprinkel. *Beyond Fundraising: New Strategies for Nonprofit Innovation and Investment* (New York: John Wiley and Sons, 1997).

Modus Ponens. Wikipedia. Accessed December 5, 2006, http://en.wikipedia.org/wiki/Modus_ponens.

"Seattle Direct Effect Industry Multipliers," RIMS Bureau of Economic Analysis (Washington: U.S. Government Printing Office, 2003).

Barton, Noelle and Holly Hall. "Special Report: A Year of Big Gains," *Chronicle of Philanthropy: The Newspaper of the Nonprofit World* (October 26, 2006, p. 8).

"Five C's of Credit." Accessed December 31, 2006, http://www.answers.com/Five%20C's%20of%20Credit.

"Regional Multipliers from the Regional Input-Output Modeling System (RIMS II): A Brief Description." Last updated March 6, 2007. Accessed March 16, 2007, http://www.bea.gov/regional/rims/brfdesc.cfm.

"Nonprofit Public Image," *Harris Interactive DonorPulse Survey,* January 2006. Accessed August 22, 2006, http://nonprofit.about.com/od/trendsissuesstatistics/a/pubopinion.htm.

"Charitable Giving Rises Six Percent to More than $20 Billion in 2005," *Giving USA*, a publication of Giving USA Foundation, researched and written by the Center on Philanthropy at Indiana University (2006).

"NCCS Quick Facts," *National Center for Charitable Statistics.* Updated May 26, 2006. Accessed February 5, 2007, http://nccsdataweb.urban.org/NCCS/files/quickFacts.htm.

# CHAPTER 2

# The Changing Philanthropic Environment

> **ADAM SMITH** *It is not from the benevolence of the butcher, the brewer, or the baker, that we expect our dinner, but from their regard to their own interest.*

## DEAD ECONOMISTS AND NONPROFITS

Adam Smith was an eighteenth-century Scottish economist, most widely known for his treatise on the motivations of individuals acting in their own self-interest as adding, not subtracting, from the broader goals of society. His second work, *An Inquiry into the Nature and Causes of the Wealth of Nations*, better known as *The Wealth of Nations*, was published in 1776, and earned him the title of the Father of Economics.

The author must admit he has never read this entire work, and is willing to bet few economists, let alone most others, have either. The modern version of the book is over 900 pages, and delves into such detail (pin making in eighteenth-century England) that its lack of complete readership is not surprising. Certain parts are somewhat amusing, such as a discussion on the number of alehouses and their relationship to drunkenness. The central points made in the book, though (I plead that the economists of the world provide a bit of artistic license), are as powerful today as they ever were.

Point 1—The pursuit of self-interest ultimately results in a better economy and a better society.

Point 2—Individuals acting in their own self-interest are "led by an invisible hand," which leads to results that ultimately benefit all and not just themselves.

These points have, through the years, been debated, modified, negated, applauded, and reiterated. Much of the original theories of the book, though, have remained valid even in today's modern postindustrial economy. The fact that much of the nonprofit world has chosen to believe that these economic truths do not apply to them is amazing.

The philanthropic environment of today, in the context of the philanthropic timeline of this country, has gone through some recent changes. Nonprofits have embraced the capability of computers and database software to expand their annual appeals. Customer relationship management (CRM) software is now in place to maximize the yield of these same campaigns. Social venturing and nonprofit entrepreneurs, people who want to provide guidance and influence rather than just money, are increasing trends. Even the tax laws regarding major gifts and estates are evolving. These changes are not what are referenced in the title of this chapter.

The changes that merit discussion are *how and why* people, foundations, and corporations *give* to nonprofits. And the word *give* itself is part of the problem. From this point forward in this book, a new vocabulary is in order, which will hopefully help change the limiting mindset unfortunately adopted by so many nonprofits.

### New Vocabulary Words

| | |
|---|---|
| Investor | One who provides funding to nonprofits. |
| Investment | Something expected to provide a return for the risk taken. Something expected to appreciate in value. Formerly known as donations, gifts, and contributions. |
| ROI | Return on investment, literally return divided by investment, or what one gets in return for providing funding. |
| NPO | Nonprofit organization. |

### Words to Expunge

| | |
|---|---|
| Donor | Traditional term for a person who contributes money to an NPO. (This is what one does with organs, not money.) |

| Gift | Something given that implies nothing is expected in return, or something received that you really didn't want or need. |
| Charity | Often synonymous with a nonprofit organization when used as a noun. |
| Nonprofit | To be used only in describing the IRS designation of the organization, not the goal. (This is so important, yet so basic, that we put it on a tee shirt; visit www.capitalstrategists.com). |

## THREE PARADIGM SHIFTS

Whenever there is a scandal in the nonprofit world, such as exorbitant executive pay or embezzlement, the popular press, pundits, and occasionally lawmakers like to suggest changes they collectively feel will mitigate the current situation and prevent it from happening again. Recently that brought us the Sarbanes-Oxley Act, which has caused words like *accountability* and *transparency* to become quite the topics of discussion.

While the shift toward accountability and transparency may itself be a paradigm shift, three other shifts are more relevant to sustainability.

### Paradigm Shift #1: Eliminating the Gift Mentality

One of the major foundations of sustainability is based on moving an organization whose funding is dependent on the grant cycle of other institutions to a mindset of investment in results by those who realize the benefit of the organization's efforts. In other words, moving it from a charity mindset, to one of investment:

Charity ⟹ Investment

To make the leap from a charity mindset to one of investment, the traditional cycle of funding used by many nonprofits must be modified. The long-term sustainability of many organizations is rooted in the lessons learned from the for-profit sector, with the primary lesson being the delivery of products or services that are valued by the market. While there is no question that most nonprofits are valuable to the community, the challenge is the demonstration, communication, and delivery of that value.

Read almost any book on fundraising and you will see a chapter, section, or maybe even the entire book on Major Gifts. This is an unfortunate choice of words, but the entire nomenclature of classical fundraising is drenched in this charity mindset. The word *gift* itself implies several things, many of which are not appropriate for the investment-driven model.

## Gift vs. Investment

| *Gift Implications* | *Investment Implications* |
| --- | --- |
| Nothing expected in return | Something expected in return |
| Small, not of major value | Large, major value |
| Social and cultural emphasis | Business emphasis |
| Better to give than receive | A penny saved is a penny earned |
| A hope that receiver will appreciate it | The expectation it will perform |

## Paradigm Shift #2: Emphasis on Results

When Capital Strategists Group is contracted to write a Sustainability Plan for an NPO, one of the sections always included is entitled *Investable Outcomes*. The reason for this is that if the investment concept is truly embraced, one can work backward from the value of the outcome being provided to what needs to happen to produce that outcome. If the future program of work is shaped by those outcomes that have the most value to potential funders, the plans can often write themselves. The emphasis is not on what output the NPO provides, but the value of the outcomes to funders. Sort of a "follow the money" strategy in reverse.

This emphasis on results is also important in moving beyond a plan to testing the plan for its funding potential. For those new to the nonprofit arena or those who have never conducted a capital campaign, raising money in a capital campaign is really a two-step process:

1. The Funding Feasibility Study
2. The Campaign

The feasibility stage is where the plan of work in need of funding is presented to potential investors for their feedback. The three questions that must be answered in a successful testing of whether a campaign should be launched are:

1. What is the NPO going to do?
2. How much will it cost?
3. What will be accomplished?

It's that third question where the emphasis on results is so important. Translated, it asks, "What's in it for me?" And the NPO had better have a good answer.

If the results of the feasibility are positive and a campaign is launched, the emphasis on results becomes even more critical. This is the point at which people, foundations, and corporations are actually being asked to write a check to the NPO. When actual money is on the line, people seem to get very interested in how their investment will be used.

## Paradigm Shift #3: The Shift Away from the Emotional Approach

This book is decidedly on the side of the nonemotional appeal. When the business approach is combined with other time-tested fundraising techniques, such as what to do in an "ask," the combination often proves extremely effective. The more one moves from left to right on the Appeal Spectrum in Exhibit 2.1, the more one is appealing to bottom line, business decision–like motivations. The further one gets to the right, the less useful the anecdotal stories become, and the more useful facts and figures are used. At the extreme right, the case is made specifically for the prospect (or their business).

An example on the extremes may provide some insight into this way of thinking. An animal rescue shelter launching a campaign, if using the appeals on the left, will focus on methods that elicit an emotional response, such as brochures that show a starving puppy. The same shelter, if using appeals on the right, will demonstrate how funding will eliminate thousands of unwanted litters and save on the costs of patrolling, sheltering, and even euthanizing. The cost of not improving the shelter that is in disrepair and how the aforementioned services show up as increased property taxes will be highlighted. The opportunity costs will demonstrate how the cost savings will more than pay for a pet park.

The areas within the spectrum present another dimension to the information used. The Output area in the middle is where statistics that

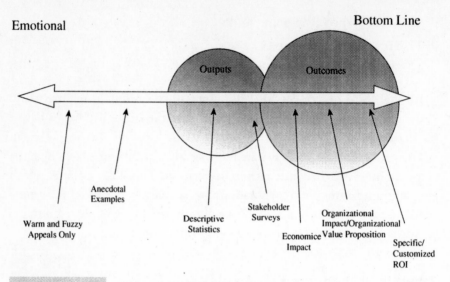

Emotional

Bottom Line

Outputs

Outcomes

Anecdotal
Examples

Stakeholder
Surveys

Organizational
Impact/Organizational
Value Proposition

Warm and Fuzzy
Appeals Only

Descriptive
Statistics

Economice
Impact

Specific/
Customized
ROI

**EXHIBIT 2.1   Appeal Spectrum**

are typically measures of activity are presented, such as how many people came to performances, received medical attention, or attended classes. While these types of statistics are a step in the right direction, they still do not go far enough. The next general area of information, Outcomes, presents the results of the Outputs, such as how many thought the performance was inspiring, the prevention value of the medical attention, or the improved graduation rate of those attending classes.

The bottom line appeal may at first glance seem too cold to be effective. Who wouldn't be moved by the starving puppies mentioned earlier? The answer is that the typical prospective investor in a nonprofit is hit with literally thousands of these appeals per year. One might get lucky and be the one chosen to be funded. What we have seen over and over again is that the investor simply divides up the "philanthropic fund" among many nonprofits, giving each so small a piece that the amount does not make much of a difference.

In her book, *The Ask: How to Ask Anyone for Any Amount for Any Reason*, Laura Fredericks list 12 main reasons why people give, as listed in Exhibit 2.2. She goes on to explain her basis for developing the list, and the nuances of the various entries.

Most of the reasons will be familiar to many people, especially those who have worked in the nonprofit arena or have given nonprofits their hard-

EXHIBIT 2.2    REASONS WHY PEOPLE GIVE

1. Belief that giving is the greatest gift of all
2. Belief that all the money in the world cannot buy happiness
3. Belief that there will always be someone less fortunate who needs money
4. Belief that charity begins at home
5. Belief that it is the right thing to do
6. Decision that accumulated assets have made it possible to give
7. Desire to emulate others who give
8. Life-transforming event, such as an accident, near-death experience, or winning the lottery
9. Guilt, especially when the money was earned or received in less desirable ways
10. Desire to reduce taxes
11. Pressure from a friend, peer, or colleague to support a cause that is important to that person
12. Need to be recognized

earned dollars. Most of them are also intuitive, and one would find it difficult to disagree with their inclusion on the list.

The reasons listed can be classified into several major categories:

- Belief systems (Reasons 1 through 5)
- Financial means (Reason 6)
- Emotions (Reasons 7 and 9)
- Dramatic event ( Reason 8)
- Tax reduction (Reason 10)
- Peer pressure (Reason 11)
- Recognition (Reason 12)

The only reason listed that is grounded purely in ROI is Reason 10, reducing one's tax burden. The reason that is conspicuously absent is what is typically asked by the crowd on the far right of the Appeal Spectrum: What's in it for me? In the traditional world of Hospitals, Colleges, and Museums (HCMs), there are plenty of emotions, affinities, and status motivations with which to work. There may not be many WIIFMs, but the smaller nonprofits are surrounded by them.

What follows in subsequent chapters are specific examples of how this approach only opens up a new category of potential investors, and how it has worked for many different types of NPOs.

## THE LEVERAGE OF ~~DONORS~~ INVESTORS

In any given concentration of people, whether small-town America or bustling metropolis, there are the usual suspects for nonprofit investment: banks, utility companies, major employers, wealthy individuals, corporate headquarters, and so on. The issue is that the same people and organizations get hit again and again with solicitations. And they are growing tired of it.

When the uninitiated nonprofit in Atlanta wants to raise money, they immediately think of Coca Cola or Home Depot or UPS as likely suspects. And why not? They know they are good corporate citizens, and that this is their corporate home. The flaw in their logic is that it is only based on the capacity of the potential investors. The truth is that these major organizations have dedicated staffs whose job it is to say "no." When wealthy individuals want to put some distance between themselves and the seemingly endless string of "asks," they hire gatekeepers or simply stop taking calls.

NPOs would do well to think as a bank does in qualifying a loan request; they do not rely on only one determinant. Banks have traditionally used the Five C's of Credit: capacity, character, capital, collateral, and conditions. Nonprofits often rely on capacity alone to qualify a potential investor; if they have money, they are a prospect. As we will discuss later, capacity is the least effective qualifier of who will invest in a nonprofit.

All of this demand for funding being funneled to the same prospects over and over again has put them in a position of being able to call the tune, and the name of the tune heard over and over is *return on investment* (ROI). Based on hundreds of personal, confidential, and one-on-one interviews during funding feasibility studies for many clients, the most common way in which this leverage is expressed is by the following three statements:

1. What's in it for me?
2. Show me something (results) I can take to my board.
3. I need to see something specific in return for my money.

# THE EVOLVING LANDSCAPE

Having worked with many types of nonprofits over a number of years, one sees trends and patterns develop that allow certain inferences to be made. One of the most positive trends seen in the last several years is the continued evolving of nonprofits in their quest for sustainability. Generally, they fall into three groups, what we term Traditional, Sustainable, and Cash Generating organizations.

## Traditional

This group includes 90 percent of the nonprofits that cross our path. They are still stuck in the charity mindset, seem to look to the government first for funding, and spend a lot of money on the flavor-of-the-month fundraising, whether it's special events, new software, or direct-mail appeals. Their reliance on grant funding is so predominant that when grant deadlines approach, everything else is put on hold and all available resources are channeled to getting that grant application out the door. (If this sounds familiar, you are probably in this category.)

This type of organization is the least likely to fully accept the message that value matters; or to be fairer, they accept it but do not act fully on it. The path of least resistance is that of continuing to rely on government funding, and they appear to believe that resources are better spent on a good grant writer than on delivering and communicating value to investors, especially private sector investors.

## Sustainable

This group is comprised of those former Traditional NPOs that finally got it. While the journey to embracing an investment-driven model may have been painful, they are now reaping the benefits. Sometimes this meant that their annual fundraising campaign had to be abandoned in favor of a multiyear strategic initiative that produced tangible outcomes. Other times it meant that membership dues based on a rather arbitrary scale needed to be based more on the member's ability to invest and the level of value received. Organizations in this group typically have a self-financing component in their program of work, and their reputation is growing because of it.

## Cash Generating

These are the valedictorians of the nonprofit class, often adopting investment-driven techniques without even knowing it or putting a name to it. The executives often have a strong entrepreneurial streak in them, and it's not unusual for them to have private sector backgrounds. They introduced sustaining elements and programs years ago, which are now generating enough cash to pay for the other programs in the organization that lose money. In some cases, they are even considering spinning off the money-making programs as for-profit companies, and even selling them so the proceeds can be plowed back into the nonprofit. In some cases, the IRS may force them to somehow restructure their operations because they may look like for-profit enterprises.

# An Unlevel Playing Field

Large, traditional nonprofits, those exemplified by hospitals, colleges, and museums—HCMs for the purpose of our discussion—have fundraising down pat. And they should. HCMs have been around for a long time, have a thoroughly researched and cultivated donor base, and a very effective set of motivations on which to capitalize. Those who will find this book most useful typically do not have this capacity or these characteristics.

Without the luxury of alumni, the emotional appeal of care when sick, or the aesthetic appeal of culture. The remaining nonprofits are at a distinct disadvantage in the competition for funding. These differences become more obvious when the characteristics are given a realistic context.

---

### TRADITIONAL HCM EXAMPLE

The hospital has been in town for years. In fact, some of the board members were born there, and so were some of their children. Large funders can drive by the building and point it out to their grandchildren, and can say they helped build it. If they are large enough funders, their family name might even be over the door of the new Cancer Treatment wing.

The list of board members reads like a *Who's Who* of the town, and there is a waiting list to be on it. Being on the board of this hospital connotes a certain status in the community, and they are proud to be members of this rather exclusive club. They understand that to be on the board takes big bucks, and that at some point they will be asked for some.

Funders understand that if they get sick, this is where they will likely go for treatment. Or that if their children get into an accident, this is the emergency room to which they will be brought.

The hospital itself is a large operation and is run by a professional staff. They touch the lives of many people every day, often in circumstances of life and death. The emotional tie of saving a life is a strong motivation to make the facility and its services as effective as possible.

## NON HCM EXAMPLE

The health network is new by comparison. They have been around for five years and were given their start by a three-year federal grant. They have a relatively small staff and an even smaller rented office, which is one of many in a converted strip mall. It is difficult to find and not in a thriving part of town.

Their board is made up of concerned people who were recruited because of their expertise and experience, not because of their capacity to provide funding. Their board is considered a "working" board.

What they do is very important to the community, but few people seem to know about them. There is little status associated with being on their board. While they feel they deserve financial support from the community, they do not have the budget, expertise, or time to embark on a funding campaign.

If these examples sound familiar, it's because they are real. In fact, they are actual situations in the very same community! To make the situation even more realistic, the HCM had a capital campaign less than three years ago that makes the other NPO feel like "They sucked up all of the money in this town." While this is probably not accurate, the feeling was commonly held to be true.

EXHIBIT 2.3    ORGANIZATIONAL TYPES AND FUNDING
DIFFERENCES

|  | Traditional HCM (Hospital, College, Museum) | Non HCM Nonprofit Organization |
| --- | --- | --- |
| Characteristics | Large; institutional | Small; little physical presence; virtual organization |
| History | Old; established | Newer; under radar |
| Motivations | Legacy (naming) Fear of negative outcome Visualize use Connection to cause Status Corporate citizen Positive outcomes Common values Social standing | Corporate citizen Fear of negative outcome Visualize use Connection to cause Positive outcomes Common values |
| Prospects | Around board table Previous funders Alumni/members Suppliers Staff Wealthy individuals | *Not* around board table Previous funders Clients/users Wealthy individuals |
| Challenges | Leadership *choices* Management of people Campaign length | Leadership *candidates* Cash flow Prospect identification |

The differences between the traditional HCM and the Non HCM NPO are summarized in Exhibit 2.3.

What can the Non HCM do to elevate its situation and put it in a position for funding? Many things come to mind, from a public relations campaign to beefing up the board to applying for even more grants. All of these actions are steps in the right direction, but take time and money, with the payoff possibly being in the distant future. The experience of working with many of these Non HCM, or those that are not HCMs, has led to many of the concepts in this book. The solution was that once they demonstrated and communicated their value to the community, and adopted an investment-driven approach to funding, they were in a much better position to invite and accept investment in their organization.

# ■ REFERENCES

Fredericks, Laura. *The Ask: How to Ask Anyone for Any Amount for Any Purpose* (San Francisco: Jossey-Bass, 2006, p. 13).

Smith, Adam. *An Inquiry Into the Nature and Causes of the Wealth of Nations*, ed. EdwinCannan (New York: Modern Library, 1937, first published in 1776).

# Organizational Reluctance

## LEARNING FROM THE FOR-PROFIT WORLD

One reason why NPOs have been reluctant to embrace more from the for-profit world is simply that they have been told, by virtue of being in the nonprofit club, that they should not. They have been inculcated from the beginning that they are different, and often in a manner that is not intended to build confidence. In many of our workshops across the country, this question is asked:

*Do your outcomes provide an acceptable level of ROI to your investors?*

Many think they are in the wrong room, since they do not have "investors." Others do not feel that the term *ROI* applies to them. Once the vernacular is explained to them, the question is asked again. Few still answer affirmatively. If this question were posed to a group of for-profit executives, one cannot imagine them not answering with a resounding "Of course they do," even if it were not actually true.

When it comes to funding, the steps involved in raising money for a nonprofit through a capital campaign and raising money for a for-profit via the capital markets are strikingly similar:

1. Make a compelling case for investment.
2. Get investors to commit.
3. Produce something they value.

In fact, many of the nuances are also similar:

- A prospectus is prepared, detailing what will be done with the money.
- Potential investors are visited before the general public is invited to invest.
- The intermediaries, fundraisers for nonprofits and investment bankers for for-profits, involved in the transaction take a significant cut of the proceeds.

Unlike the for-profit world in which metrics abound, many nonprofit executives lament that they have no objective criteria on which to be evaluated by the general public. While they are often evaluated within the context of individual grants, these are usually below the general public's level of interest. Nonprofit executives often feel that none of the following, which are common in the "real" world, apply to their situation:

- Profit
- Market share
- Return on equity
- Share price
- Number of locations
- Profit margin
- Market capitalization
- Number of units sold

These nonprofit executives are correct in that none of the aforementioned directly apply to the nonprofit world. They have the advantage of being able to define their respective metrics within their own mission. This allows for a better framing of the ROI discussion and a somewhat easier time of determining the proper metrics. It also affords nonprofits a huge advantage that is not shared by their for-profit counterparts: Not only will people pay for your products or services; they will also give you money to support your broader mission!

Many grants have a built-in evaluation component, which is to say that some of the money must be dedicated to proving that the grantor's money is spent as they intended it to be. These evaluation instruments are all too often cloaked in industry jargon and make no sense to outsiders simply trying to determine if the NPO is delivering outcomes they value. For example, these phrases are taken directly from evaluation reports from actual NPOs, and are intended to convey the facts that the NPO actually accomplished something:

"Served as a neutral party in fostering collaborative partnerships."

"Acted in the capacity of lead agency for selected initiatives."

"Assumed the role of catalyst for pursuing regional responses."

Can the average reader, whether on the board or a potential investor, make any sense of such consultant-speak? The outsider is still left with the unanswered question, "What did you accomplish?" One must consider that if it is this difficult to determine what the respective NPO does, it is doubly hard to figure out if they are doing a good job.

## FIVE CLASSIC FUNDRAISING MISCONCEPTIONS

Organizational reluctance is also evidenced by the clichés often heard in nonprofit circles. The original title of this section was "Five Classic Fundraising Myths," but that implied that they had a strong probability of being false. The fact is, they are not false, just no longer appropriate when ROI is introduced correctly.

### 1. Nonprofits Cannot Be Run Like a Business

The following quote appears on the top of an invitation to subscribe to *The Nonprofit Quarterly*, a publication of the Nonprofit Information Networking Association:

We must reject the idea—well intentioned, but dead wrong—that the primary path to greatness in the social sectors is to become more like a business.

This quote is attributed to Jim Collins, author of *Built to Last* and *Good to Great*. He also wrote a nonprofit companion to *Good to Great* entitled *Good to Great and the Social Sectors*. A quote taken out of context like this can unfortunately lead one to the wrong conclusion. If the entire book is read, the reader will see that Mr. Collins's theories and this book's ideas do not disagree; they, in fact, support each other.

Although some paths to greatness may still be elusive, the knowledge and tools necessary are attainable for nonprofits that are struggling every day to accomplish their funding missions. The truth is that a nonprofit is a business, whether one philosophically agrees with this or not. The quote at the beginning of this chapter says it all: Nonprofit is a designation, not a goal.

Characteristics of a business, whether designated by the IRS as for-profit or nonprofit, broadly include revenue, expenses, and what is left when the latter is subtracted from the former. In the for-profit world, what is left is profit or loss. While the nonprofit world does not use the term *profit*, they seem quite comfortable in adopting the term *loss*. Both classifications pay employees, have boards or oversight committees, and provide a product or service. Both will cease to exist if they operate in the red for too long.

Those on the far right of this issue will say that it is precisely the differences, which are arguably small, that do not allow a nonprofit to be run like a business. Each day this issue continues to be debated is one more day nonprofits waste on philosophy rather than producing results.

## 2. People Give to People, Not Causes

A 26-year veteran of the fundraising arena and a personal friend the author greatly respects, George Pfeiffer, once said, "Perhaps this is an over-simplification." People do give to people. They also give to causes. Let me restate this simplification:

1.  People give more to the right person.
2.  People give more to the right cause.
3.  People give the most when the right person with the right cause are combined.

Why not fire on all cylinders and give them both?

Any book on Fundraising 101 will tell you that a peer-to-peer solicitation is most effective. The solicitor must be the same as or slightly above the solicitee in some contributory, socioeconomic, or societal fashion. If prospects are giving only because the right person asked them, the only motivation being employed is personal credibility of the person doing the asking; it completely ignores the good work done by the organization.

This situation often becomes a vicious philanthropic cycle in a given locality when it devolves into simply swapping checks from one organization to the next. The conversation typically goes something like this:

Bob: "Bill, remember last year when you asked me for $50,000 to help the new Community Center?"

Bill: "Sure I do. Without your help, it wouldn't have been a success."

Bob: "Well, this year I'm in charge of the campaign to build the new cancer wing at the hospital. Can I count on you to help us out at the same level?

Bill: "Well, money is kind of tight this year."

Bob: "C'mon Bill, it was tight last year when I helped you out."

Bill: "Okay Bob, I'm only doing it because we're friends."

This scenario does raise money, and does get a nonprofit funded. However, it could easily be three or four times that amount if the cause was:

1. Something with which Bill had a connection

2. Something that touched a motivation besides friendship

3. Couched in terms that demonstrated the value of his investment in the community in terms he understood and appreciated

## 3. We Are Doing God's Work

The implications here are that because one is doing God's work—feeding the poor or tending to the sick—demonstrating ROI is not important. Stated differently, people will not need to see value to be convinced to invest in an organization doing God's work.

With scandals involving executive pay and misappropriation of funds at some of the largest NPOs in the country not uncommon, this misconception is losing some steam. Even the most charitable of charities now realize that they must demonstrate to their constituency that they are using funds judiciously and effectively.

### 4. ROI Does Not Belong in a Nonprofit

When we started preaching the gospel of nonprofit ROI in 1992, we were accused of committing nonprofit blasphemy. The audacity of suggesting that a nonprofit be expected to demonstrate ROI was not well received. "It's not even possible to do it!" they exclaimed. My, how things have changed.

Even if one does not consider how our business has grown, which could be viewed as biased, the fact that most grant applications now contain a section entitled "Expected Impacts" or "Outcomes to be Achieved" is evidence enough that the concept is now widely accepted.

### 5. ROI Is Not a Motivation for My Donor Base

The response to this is very straightforward; if you believe this, then you are leaving huge amounts of money on the table. If you are only firing on the cylinders of emotional appeal, you are not engaging the larger universe of potential investors.

This response is most often heard from nonprofits engaged in the human services area. They are quick to use images of children and people obviously in need. These images are very effective, and play on emotions very well. At the basic level, those who would invest in this cause do not need to be shown ROI; the ROI is in eliminating human suffering.

But let's go to the next level. When a nonprofit investor is faced with a choice of investing in an NPO with a demonstrated track record of effectiveness versus one who basically says, "Just trust me," which choice will the investor make?

## MORE ON "PEOPLE GIVE TO PEOPLE, NOT CAUSES"

This mantra is so prevalent in the fundraising world that it deserves special attention. In the many discussions with those who have been in the nonprofit arena many years, George Pfeiffer again put it so well:

> The essential principle I learned in my years of nonprofit work is that people give to people, they don't give to causes. Perhaps this is an oversimplification, but like many principles that need some clarification, it makes the underlying point very clear. Solicitations are most successful

when the solicitor is at least a peer and enjoys the respect of the one being solicited. Clearly, the cause must not violate the values of the solicitee, and must be perceived as making some positive impact. But, as all of us experience every day, there is a myriad of good causes wanting our attention and support. The requests we most likely will respond positively to, are those which are personal, are compatible with those issues we believe are important, and are made by a person we respect.

These points cannot be argued, and have been proven time and time again in all manners of nonprofit. But let me give another scenario. Joe gives to Ducks Unlimited, a nonprofit headquartered in Memphis, Tennessee. He does not hunt ducks. He does not know anyone who works for Ducks Unlimited. He has never been personally approached by anyone associated with Ducks Unlimited. Sometimes they even misspell his name on the various marketing materials they send him. He still sends them $50 every year.

Joe is living proof that "People give to people, not causes" is not exactly true. The reason is that Ducks Unlimited is conducting an annual campaign, and the personal solicitations referenced in the previous quote refer to a capital campaign.

Annual campaigns depend on a different set of motivations than capital campaigns do. While the motivations are discussed in depth in Chapter 4, the point here is that Joe gives because he understands that Ducks Unlimited spends much of their money on wetlands conservation. They let him know several times a year how many dollars they are spending, how many acres they are preserving, and how many more ducks are hatching because of their efforts. This is the technical ROI they are providing him. His $50 a year, and the $50 of thousands of other people every year, provide the results on an economy of scale that could not be done otherwise.

However, it goes deeper than that. Joe simply likes to see the ducks fly overhead in the fall. He likes the sound they make, and the natural signal that winter is coming. In fact, he is seeing more and more ducks every year. He is thinking about doubling his annual investment to $100. Bottom line: They are providing him a tangible ROI he can see, hear, and read about.

To be sure, the larger the dollar amount being solicited, the more a personal solicitation comes into play. The fact remains that people *do* give to causes. If that cause is justified by a strong ROI, they will give even more.

# MORE ON "NONPROFITS CAN'T BE RUN LIKE A BUSINESS"

The Jim Collins quote discussed earlier, that "We must reject the idea . . . that the primary path to greatness in the social sectors is to become 'more like a business'," is easy to take out of context. This is the first line of his monograph, *Good to Great and the Social Sectors*, a companion to his best selling *Good to Great*. This perspective, as introduced in the book, was met with disagreement by almost everyone in the room full of business leaders where he was speaking.

A CEO in attendance went on to explain that the nonprofits he was familiar with could use more discipline in planning, allocation of resources, and so on. Mr. Collins's response was, "What makes you think that's a *business* concept?" His point is that "a culture of discipline is not a principle of business; it is a principle of greatness."

Many NPO executives claim that nonprofits cannot use the same metrics to measure performance as for-profits, and Generally Accepted Accounting Principles (GAAP) would agree with this. However, as Mr. Collins states, this is "simply a lack of discipline." Meaningful metrics can be developed in the social sector, but they will not be universally comparable as they are in the for-profit world. The missions of NPOs are too different to lend themselves to a narrow set of measures like profit or earnings per share. However, they can be developed, and when done correctly often lead to greater funding.

# SUCCESS LEAVES CLUES

The corporate model of the capitalistic world has been successful, especially in this country. The field of investment banking seems to draw some of the best and brightest minds from the most prestigious universities. Why? Because the system works, and there is a lot of money to be made.

The "Goal of the Firm," as stated in most finance textbooks, is to *maximize shareholder wealth*. The subtleties of each word are important here. *Maximize* connotes that something should be made the most of, or taken to the extreme. *Shareholder* indicates that only those who are considered owners have a right to the return, since they are taking the risk. *Wealth* implies a long-term outlook, measured over years, as opposed to income, which implies short-term gains.

When large groups of nonprofits in various instructive sessions are asked, "What is the goal of your firm?" typical answers are:

- To fulfill our mission
- To help as many as we can
- To operate efficiently and do our job
- To make a difference
- To make our community a better place to live
- To eliminate suffering

These are great answers, and one would hesitate to change any of them. However, can the way in which these goals are accomplished be improved? Can the way in which the organizations themselves are funded be improved? Yes they can, and the clues left by the corporate world have proven to be very applicable in doing this.

## FEAR OF "PUTTING YOUR MISSION UP FOR SALE"

A smaller part of the reluctance of organizations to adopt an investment-driven approach to sustainability is that they feel in doing so they would be prostituting their mission. No one is suggesting that an NPO's mission be sold to the highest bidder, but this line of thinking is not uncommon. A snappy retort from the other side of the issue is, "No margin, no mission." Philosophy aside, there is a happy medium in this discussion.

Any NPO that has raised money through a capital campaign knows that the first step is the testing of the idea, more commonly known as a *funding feasibility study*. In this process, likely suspects are typically interviewed to determine their potential support for the initiative at hand. Having been involved in literally thousands of these interviews over the last dozen or so years, the author has first-hand knowledge of the wide array of responses given in these interviews. A typical exchange goes something like this:

Interviewer:     Does this project fit within your area of interest?
Interviewee:     It seems to fit well.
Interviewer:     Is it something you could support financially, say at the
                 $100,000 level?

| | |
|---|---|
| Interviewee: | I could support it even more if you put more resources behind the Community Health (example) portion. |
| Interviewer: | How much more are we talking about? |
| Interviewee: | I'd consider a million dollars if they would institute a worksite wellness program. That makes sense from my company's point of view. |
| Interviewer: | There are no worksite wellness provisions in the program now, but its inclusion can certainly be discussed. |

Is the NPO putting its mission up for sale if it expands its initiative to include a worksite wellness program? Not if its mission contains phrases such as "improve overall community health" or "improve the health status of all county residents." Delivering outcomes that are valued by funders is not prostituting one's mission or putting one's mission up for sale. It is simply delivering results that investors value.

■ **REFERENCES**

Invitation to subscribe to *The Nonprofit Quarterly* (Boston: Nonprofit Information Networking Association, 2006).

Pfeiffer, George. Interview faxed on October 26, 2006.

Collins, Jim. *Good to Great and the Social Sectors: A Monograph to Accompany Good to Great.* (Boulder: Jim Collins, 2005).

# CHAPTER 4

# Organizational Change

> **HERRINGTON J. BRYCE** *An economic institution creates something of value. The assumption ... is that nonprofits have measurable economic value—even if the measure is imperfect.*

## MOVING TO AN INVESTMENT-BASED MINDSET

An early experience with a particular fundraiser was unique in that they had just begun using a direct solicitation model, rather than a volunteer-driven model. It couldn't have been a better learning experience. Most fundraising has traditionally been volunteer-driven, that is to say that people within the NPO, board members, committee members, and staff, shouldered the burden of actual solicitations. The announcement of an organization launching a capital campaign was often met with groans by both the board and staff, since they knew how much work it involved.

The volunteer model of fundraising did not lend itself to an investment-driven mindset because of the structure of the model itself. It employs a sort of multilevel marketing approach that takes a lot of time and people. Many refer to this as the "coaching," and sometimes the "cheerleading" model, depending on their distaste for the methods. It typically involves gathering people in a room, briefing them on how to approach their peers, associates, or targeted list of prospects, giving them a pep talk, and unleashing them on the community. When that particular group raised the requisite amount of money, other groups were dispatched, until the money was raised.

The late 1980s and early 1990s ushered in a new model that was my first exposure to the intricacies of a capital campaign, and the advantages of a professional solicitation model. In this model, outside professionals are used to make the actual "ask." It has many advantages, such as a more consistent message, less strain on personal relationships, and less staff time. As you can imagine, it also costs more initially, but it does produce impressive results.

The volunteer model, with its dependence on relationships, emotional appeals, and often arm-twisting, does not need to adopt an investment-driven approach to be successful. The professional solicitation model, since it relies less on personal relationships, is almost forced to adopt an investment-driven mindset. Being repeatedly asked, "What's in it for me?" serves to hone the answer, since no money is raised if the answer is not satisfactory.

## NONPROFIT VS. FOR-PROFIT MODELS

The nonprofit funding model and the for-profit funding model are very similar in the early stages (see Exhibits 4.1 and 4.2). They both see a need, secure funding, and fill that need. That is where the similarities end. After seeing a need, the nonprofit organization, or NPO, typically writes a grant. If the grant application is funded, the NPO goes about spending the funds and filling the need. The disruption in the funding cycle occurs when the grant runs out, or must be reapplied for on a continual basis. This is the situation faced by many NPOs.

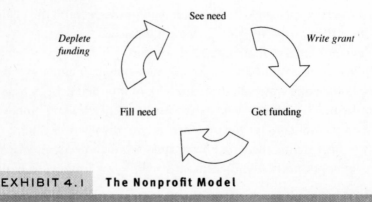

*Deplete funding* · See need · *Write grant* · Fill need · Get funding

EXHIBIT 4.1    **The Nonprofit Model**

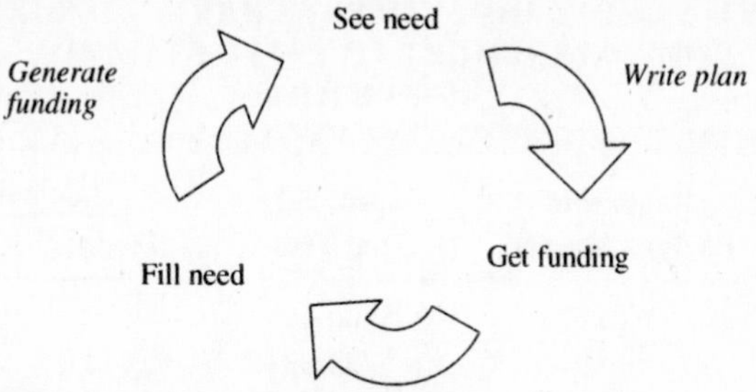

See need

Generate
funding

Write plan

Fill need

Get funding

**EXHIBIT 4.2    The For-Profit Model**

Conversely, the for-profit model does not have the opportunity to participate in the grant process. If, in the process of filling the need, they do not do it in such a way that allows the product or service to pay for itself, and generate a fair profit, the marketplace will put them out of business.

NPOs are very good at filling the need, but are often less adept at:

1. Demonstrating the value of their services
2. Communicating that value in a way that is understood, at a fundamental economic level, that makes sense to the private sector

If this demonstration and communication gap can be bridged, the private sector can then be cultivated to become investors in the NPO that provides something of value to them.

## MOVING UP THE MOTIVATIONAL PYRAMID

Many fundraising books make reference to an Investor Pyramid. Usually this refers to the investment chart used in a funding feasibility study to demonstrate to potential investors the pattern of investments needed to meet the fundraising goal. It is a good reality check in that it demonstrates how the pattern of giving must play out in terms of the number of investors and at what level they must invest. It's a very useful tool to show that one or two large investors do not make a campaign, and conversely that without lead investors, the campaign will be much smaller in terms of dollars raised. An example of an investment chart is presented in Exhibit 4.3.

The pyramid that is much more revealing in an ROI context is the *motivational pyramid*. This idea of levels of attributes or motivations was first

| EXHIBIT 4.3 | SAMPLE INVESTMENT CHART: REQUIRED LEVELS OF INVESTMENT TO RAISE $15.5 MILLION IN A 3-YEAR PLEDGE PERIOD |
| --- | --- |

| Pledge Amount | Number of Pledges Needed | Amount per Year | Cumulative Totals | |
| --- | --- | --- | --- | --- |
| | | | Pledges | Amount |
| $1,500,000 | 1 | $500,000 | 1 | $1,500,000 |
| $1,000,000 | 1 | $333,333 | 2 | $2,500,000 |
| $750,000 | 2 | $250,000 | 4 | $4,000,000 |
| $500,000 | 3 | $166,667 | 7 | $5,500,000 |
| $300,000 | 5 | $100,000 | 12 | $7,000,000 |
| $200,000 | 10 | $66,667 | 22 | $9,000,000 |
| $150,000 | 15 | $50,000 | 37 | $11,250,000 |
| $100,000 | 20 | $33,333 | 57 | $13,250,000 |
| $60,000 | 38 | $20,000 | 95 | $15,530,000 |
| **Totals** | **95** | | | **$15,530,000** |

introduced to the author in concept by Kay Sprinkel Grace's book *Beyond Fundraising*. In it, she refers to three types of attributes or motivations that must be developed for effective fundraising: connection, concern, and capacity.

Connection    Described as the strongest factor in determining the potential investment, it is an emotional connection with the NPO. Example: a patient whose life was saved at the hospital, or a child who was rescued from an abusive situation.

Concern    More intellectual than emotional, this motivation is one of identifying with an NPO or its mission without being emotionally attached. Example: a corporation that invests in arts and culture organizations so that the community is more appealing, thereby making the attraction of quality employees easier.

Capacity    Not really a motivation but a qualifying characteristic, this is simply the ability to give. Example: a wealthy family that may have no connection or concern for a given NPO, or a company that is solicited because they are located in the general vicinity of the NPO.

In the investment-driven model, it helps to think of these levels in pyramid form, as in Exhibit 4.4. The pyramid concept is useful in

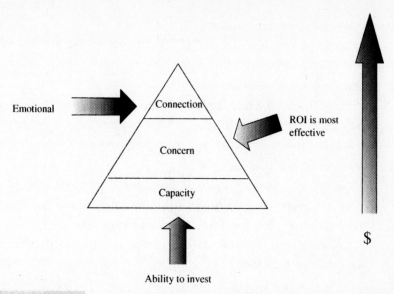

**EXHIBIT 4.4    The Motivational Pyramid**

demonstrating the concept that each level is built on the other, and as one gets to the top, the investments become larger. In other words, the largest investments are likely to come from those at the connection level, but there will be fewer of them. There will be many in number at the capacity level, but their investments will be relatively small. The Investor Chart in Exhibit 4.3 is the numerical representation of this very fact.

What is probably obvious at this point is that an ROI-based approach works best with those at the concern level. This intellectual rather than emotional level is literally asking for ROI, and as long as it is supplied in a credible way, the investment often follows. Examples of this in practice are presented in Chapter 10, with Case Study 8 being a good illustration of how effective this can be.

The bulk of the time spent in the trenches in the early stages of a campaign is getting those at the concern level moved up to the connection level. Many times, the early discussions focus on the concern level and how the program or organization can provide a solution, and do it in such a way that it provides an acceptable ROI. Once this level is satisfied, a la Maslow's Hierarchy of Needs, it is possible to move them up to the connection level and secure an even larger investment. We have found that the reason an investment-driven approach works so well at the concern level falls into four major categories:

1. It can quantify their intuition.

    Prospects often feel that the NPO does good work; they just need some quantification to validate it.

2. It provides the needed objectivity.

    Prospects that are bombarded with requests need some evidence that a given NPO can deliver on what they promise. A credible ROI presentation is that evidence, and needs to be objective to be credible.

3. It represents due diligence.

    When "asks" are large enough, they often get kicked upstairs and become a board-level decision in the corporate world, or a group decision in a personal foundation situation. An "ask" that is accompanied by a demonstration of value can provide the due diligence that is required at the higher levels of investment.

4. Their homework is already done.

    Believe it or not, savvy nonprofit investors do not always take a fundraiser's word on how good their nonprofit is, or that a particular cause satisfies all the prospects' needs and desires. Prospects actually do their own research and make their own evaluation of possible alternatives. A good starting point for their research should be the NPO's own ROI. This steers the prospect in the right direction, and lets them get farther along in less time.

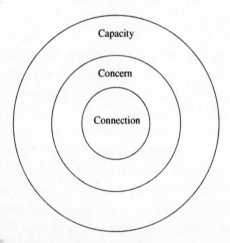

**EXHIBIT 4.5    The Motivation Target**

Another way of looking at the three levels of motivation is in concentric circles, which has a deliberate resemblance to a target (see Exhibit 4.5). This form demonstrates that the connection level is indeed the bull's eye, and that not hitting the bull's eye makes success difficult, no matter how successful one is at the other levels.

The concentric-circles approach better represents the interrelatedness of these three areas, and demonstrates that connection is encompassed by the universe of those with a concern, which is in turn encompassed by those with capacity.

The organizational changes seen by virtue of being in the nonprofit industry have also become apparent to others outside the industry. Again, from Jim Collins's *Good to Great and the Social Sectors*:

> Whereas in business, the key driver in the flywheel is the link between financial success and capital resources, I'd like to suggest that a key link in the social sectors is brand reputation—built upon tangible results and emotional share of heart—so that potential supporters believe not only in your mission, but in your capacity to deliver on that mission.

This is exactly what the connection and the concern levels speak to. The ability to deliver on that mission is what demonstrating ROI is all about.

## ▓ REFERENCES

Collins, Jim. *Good to Great and the Social Sectors: A Monograph to Accompany Good to Great* (Boulder: Jim Collins, 2005).

Grace, Kay Sprinkel. *Beyond Fundraising: New Strategies for Nonprofit Innovation and Investment* (New York: John Wiley and Sons, 1997).

# CHAPTER 5

# Organizational Value/
# Nonprofit ROI

| | |
|---|---|
| **AUTHOR UNKNOWN** | *If you can't measure it, it's art.* |

## BEYOND LOGIC MODELS—MOVING FROM OUTCOMES TO OUTCOME VALUE

Years ago, some consultant invented something called a logic model. Despite the best efforts of many people, the person who introduced it or even when it was first applied could not be determined. What can be definitively stated is that it is a requirement of many grant applications, that many nonprofit experts include it in their reports, and it is taught in "certified" nonprofit courses. The typical logic model is shown in Exhibit 5.1.

The purpose behind this is extremely instructive, since it forces one to relate a particular action to the result it produces. This sort of direct linkage is important from both a strategic planning and transparency perspective: It allows outside funders to see how their investment is being put to use.

Inputs are the resources and materials the organization uses to produce results. Inputs usually take the form of people, money, equipment, supplies, time, and so on. Budgets can be thought of as a list of inputs. To use a manufacturing analogy, inputs are the raw material of the entire process.

Outputs are typically defined as the tangible results of the program or process, and are usually described quantitatively, such as number of visits to a

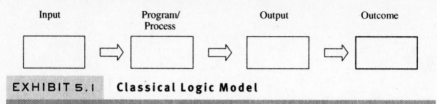

**EXHIBIT 5.1    Classical Logic Model**

free clinic, number of students attending classes, or number receiving nutritional meals. Common measurements used to describe outputs fall into categories such as throughput, activity, and attendance. Outputs are usually poor indicators of performance, since they often reflect what the organization is doing (an activity), rather than what it is accomplishing (the impact).

Outcomes are the impact on those people or conditions the organization desires to improve, and are a bit more difficult to quantify. This difficulty may be the reason why so many organizations stop at the output level: Outputs are far easier to measure. They are also less meaningful to society. For example, let's look more closely at a program designed to identify high-school dropouts and shepherd them through a program that ultimately results in a GED certificate, also known as an equivalency diploma. Made possible from a foundation grant, 200 people enter the program, and 100 successfully pass the exam and receive their GED certificate. At one level, the 100 students who successfully complete the program could be described as the outcome, as in Exhibit 5.2.

Many grant proposals and follow-up reports actually look like this. The 200 students who entered the program are easy to account for, and in this case, the 100 successful students are relatively easy to measure also. One simply has to count how many certificates are awarded. More legitimately, the 100 who pass the GED exam should be considered outputs of the program, with the outcome being the desired impact on society.

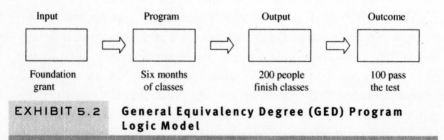

**EXHIBIT 5.2    General Equivalency Degree (GED) Program Logic Model**

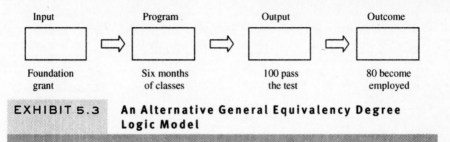

| Input | Program | Output | Outcome |
|---|---|---|---|
| Foundation grant | Six months of classes | 100 pass the test | 80 become employed |

**EXHIBIT 5.3**  **An Alternative General Equivalency Degree Logic Model**

The outcomes in this example are more difficult to track, and usually take more time and money to accurately do so. The desired outcome may be that 80 percent of these graduates become employed, or go beyond this and expect that 20 percent go on to graduate college, as in Exhibit 5.3. The difficulty is that college graduation is at least four years down the road, and it will take time and money to track their progress. Funders often want results sooner than that.

To truly embrace the investment-based model for long-term sustainability, organizations must move beyond this model and add one more step: the *value* of the outcomes (see Exhibit 5.4).

This value of $2 million injected into the local economy can be transformed into many other forms, depending on the particular audience and what they appreciate:

| *Audience* | *Value They Appreciate* |
|---|---|
| County commissioners | Increased tax base |
| Local employers | Larger labor pool |
| Local businesses | More goods and services sold |

When one can translate each of these categories into actual dollars and cents, such as how much more will be paid in property taxes or the increase in groceries purchased, the list of potential organizational funders grows dramatically.

Outcomes can be useful to the uninformed outside observer, but they might not be completely understood. For example, a community health network that spends much of its budget on education may have great outcomes, but the values of those outcomes are what are more understandable to the public at large:

| Program | Output | Outcome | Value |
|---------|--------|---------|-------|
| Six months of classes | 100 pass the test | 80 become employed | 80 jobs × $25,000 = $2 million in new earnings injected into the local economy |

EXHIBIT 5.4     The Logic Model with Value Added

| Type of Organization | Community Health Network | |
|---|---|---|
| Programs | A. | In-school prevention programs |
| | B. | Worksite wellness programs |
| Activities | A. | Health education fairs |
| | | Healthy practices taught in the classroom |
| | B. | Workplace education programs |
| | | Organizing lunch workouts |
| | | Motivating for results |
| Outputs | A. | Number of classes taught |
| | | Numbers of students touched |
| | | Amount of collateral material distributed |
| | B. | Number of people enrolled |
| | | Number of employers enrolled |
| Outcomes | A. | Fewer missed days of school |
| | | Less classroom instruction missed |
| | B. | Fewer sick days |
| | | Higher productivity |
| | | Lower health insurance premiums |

Most NPOs seem to stop there, and that is unfortunate. There is so much value to be unlocked and communicated to potential funders. Going to the next level, presented next for just one area of these outcomes, would provide so much more motivation for an investor.

## Value of Outcomes Example

Health costs are a major expense in any size company's budget. They manifest themselves in many ways, and just a few are presented here:

- Missing work because of sickness
- Lower productivity because a parent had to take a child to the doctor
- Higher insurance premiums because of a relatively unhealthy workforce
- Higher medical costs because of improper or inadequate health screening

The programs of (insert nonprofit), from worksite wellness to school obesity programs to healthier restaurant menus, all ultimately work to lessen the cost of health care to the region. Just how much can this mean, in dollars and cents, to XYZ County's economy?

One way to look at this issue is to create a reasonable workplace scenario and apply actual figures to arrive at a realistic estimate. According to the New York State Department of Labor, the largest private employment sector in XYZ County, in terms of total wages, is the manufacturing sector. With 2,174 in average annual employment (2004), and $77,786,882 in total annual wages (2004), the following scenario can be created:

1. With 250 working days per year, it could be expected that a parent would miss at least two days per year per sick child (trips to the doctor, staying home to provide care). For a family of two school-age children, this equates to four days of work missed per year, not including the days that might be missed if the parent was actually ill.

2. Four days missed per year is 1.6% of the total working days per year.

3. Applying this 1.6% to the $77 million in just the manufacturing sector alone yields $1.245 million in lost wages per year.

4. If this same 1.6% lost productivity figure is applied to all the economic sectors of XYZ County, over $9.3 million in wages are effectively lost.

This scenario is not intended to be definitive in estimating economic impact. One must realize that not all workers have two school-age children, that some costs are covered by paid sick leave, and so on. In some ways, though, the impact can be expected to be even larger. Applying an economic earnings multiplier of just 1.95 (typical to the manufacturing sector in the northeastern United States) to the earnings lost in just the manufacturing sector alone, the $1.245 million actually has a ripple effect of $2.43 million each year in lost earnings.

The values of the outcomes are more easily relatable to those outside the organization. Since $1.25 million is a big number in such a small county. In fact, our experience has shown that it is often the only factor that will allow an outside funder to invest at a substantial level. Getting to the value level serves the purpose of forcing organizations to think about their efforts from an outside perspective: the check writer.

## THE SILVER BULLET SYNDROME

ROI is not a silver bullet. By itself, it will not bring in one dollar of funding. Alone, it will not keep your investors happy. One cannot solve a nonprofit management problem with an ROI answer. No matter how good, logical, or compelling a respective case for support may be, it can be easily trumped by lack of credibility, unbelievable numbers, or the inability to explain it.

Several examples can be very instructive:

*The fundraiser who doesn't know how to explain it.* Our company supplies ROI information to fundraisers who work across the country. Without sounding stereotypical, fundraisers are usually good at organizing meetings, are pleasant to talk to, and are good at instilling a level of confidence (the good ones at least). Our experience has been that they are not what you would call *numbers people*. That's probably why the quantitatively challenged hire firms like ours.

Our work is used to help strengthen their case statement and provide the "armor-piercing ammunition" for specific solicitations. They tell us what they want to demonstrate, we tell them what data we need to do a credible job, they try their best to get it to us, and we go from there. It is a simple process that can go wrong when the explainers do not take the time to understand it before they try to convince someone else with it. It is the numeric equivalent of giving them a loaded gun and they end up shooting themselves with it.

For example, an NPO engaged in the economic development arena had a Chairman of the Board who was also the CEO of the local hospital. His influence on the rest of the board was powerful. He personally wanted to see the beds of the hospital filled, so he wanted population growth to be the basis of the ROI case. The reality of the situation is that while it is not unusual for personal agendas to creep into nonprofit management, the goal of the nonprofit was not to necessarily increase the population, but to help create jobs.

While the case could be made for the "population creates jobs" premise, it was a complicated message and took a considerable background in economics to explain it. Without the ability to effectively explain such a complicated case, the ROI becomes relatively useless.

*Using numbers that are not believable.* Presenting numbers that seem too good to be true undermines the credibility of everything else being said. The very first time our company was asked to do an analysis of a nonprofit's outcomes in 1993, the result was a 17-to-1 return for the community. With results like that, why wouldn't everyone continue to invest? While the results were accurate, quite a bit of education needs to accompany a statement such as this.

Another occasion of unbelievable numbers was the aftermath of a service often sold to nonprofits and for-profits alike: visioning. Visioning is the process of imagining where one wants the organization to go, unencumbered by that thing called reality. It often shows up at board retreats and strategic planning meetings. We were called upon to translate the results of the visioning exercise into a case for support.

The key benchmark of the community vision was to improve the local economy, stating emphatically that the average private-sector job will exceed the U.S. average by the year 2000. How could anyone not agree with this, a rising tide raising all boats and so on? The year was 1995, and the objective seemed noble, so we took it on. The actual process used is presented in a Chapter 10 case study, but the bottom line is that it was an impossible goal. What sounded like a goal the entire community could rally around was actually destined to make the NPO in charge of effectuating that goal a failure before it even started.

*Mistaking ROI as marketing.* Return on investment reports can be used in marketing, but they are not a substitute for marketing. When a multiyear pledge period campaign concludes, we are often asked to provide midterm ROI reports that provide an objective assessment of what has been accomplished. The usual venue is at an annual dinner/meeting or board retreat, and the reception is usually good, even if the information in the report is less than flattering.

Major investors and boards are usually in touch with the nonprofit's situation, and a candid analysis is what is sought. The general public, however, is usually not familiar with the nonprofit's situation, and can easily take information out of context. While a competent ROI analysis provides great information for inclusion in investor relations reports and marketing material, when it is used in total *as* marketing material, it is easily misconstrued or misunderstood.

*Assuming one size fits all.* Banks are not manufacturers. Professional service firms are not health providers. Young professionals are not retirees. The answer that satisfies one will not satisfy another.

Assuming that one version of ROI would satisfy everyone is what got a funding campaign in trouble in Tennessee. As in most campaigns, whether large or small, rural or urban, one particular company had to be involved in the early leadership or the campaign would not get off the ground. This particular company was in the poultry processing business, and was one of the largest employers in the area.

One of the goals of the organization conducting the campaign was to recruit more businesses to the area to provide more jobs, which of course has large populist appeal. Some standard ROI calculations were done, showing how the hoped-to-be-created jobs would impact the community and the economic benefit would ripple throughout the area (an example of this methodology is shown in Chapter 8). When presented to the large employer in question, it was the absolute wrong thing to say.

This particular employer viewed more jobs, and possibly higher-paying jobs, as a threat to their workforce. Basically, they were afraid that some of their workers would go across the street to a new employer for anything over a nickel an hour, and they were probably right. Why would they invest in a plan that would hurt them by driving up labor costs? They wouldn't, and they shouldn't.

The solution to this problem was not to be found in schmoozing, arm twisting, or nice lunches, but in pure economics. When the employer was shown that the labor pool would be made larger by the efforts of the nonprofit, therefore benefiting them, they became one of the lead investors and the campaign was a success. This methodology is also presented as a case study in Chapter 10.

## DEFINING ROI

The term *return on investment* (ROI) comes from the world of finance, and was traditionally used solely for discussions of for-profit concerns. In fact, most finance texts do not even use the broad term *ROI*, choosing instead to use more specific terms like *return on equity* and *return on assets*. According to the *Dictionary of Finance and Investment Terms* definition,

> Return on invested capital, usually termed *return on investment*, or *ROI*, is a useful means of comparing companies, or corporate divisions, in terms of efficiency of management and viability of product lines.

In its simplest form, ROI is

$$\frac{\text{Return}}{\text{Investment}}$$

Applying this formulaic process to what nonprofits do is really pushing the envelope. Or is it? Obtaining a value for the denominator, investment, is easy and can usually be pulled from annual budgets. The devil is in the numerator, return, and is where 95 percent of the work is done.

The value of the return can take many shapes, and the most common, based on the many nonprofits we have worked with over the years, are those such as:

- Value of direct jobs created
- Value of indirect jobs created
- Value of direct earnings
- Value of indirect earnings
- Value of capital investment

- Value of additional tax base created
- Value of additional property tax
- Value of additional consumer spending
- Value of increased earning potential
- Value of corporate relocations
- Value of local corporate expenditures
- Value of medical services provided
- Value of emergency room visits reduced
- Value of disease prevention
- Value of sick days avoided
- Value of increased productivity
- Value of medical services otherwise unavailable
- Value of increased graduation rates
- Value of increased skill in the labor pool
- Value of decreased adolescent pregnancies
- Value of lower crime rates
- Value of premature births avoided
- Value of adequate prenatal care
- Value of day care provided
- Value of medical transportation care provided
- Value of housing education classes
- Value of total entity impact (educational institution, corporation, and nonprofit)
- Value of new technical programs via their graduates
- Value of increased graduate earning potential
- Value of temporary housing provided
- Value of community neighborhood revitalization

## VALUING VALUES

Can values actually be valued? Yes, they can, but let's ease into the discussion. Tangible things are easy to value: homes, cars, real estate. Items considered commodities—that is, they become so standardized and/or common that they compete only on a price basis—are even easier to value, and have a continuous and constant market price. Even the most personal of things are valued, and insurance companies do it every day. They tell you how much your career is worth, your injury is worth, and even how much your life is worth. These values, while they are the basis of many a lawsuit and even more disagreements, are fairly straightforward in their calculations.

As one gets into the more esoteric areas of valuation, the range of accepted values becomes the subject of more discussion. In each case, though, a dollar figure is ultimately placed on an event or situation.

**Scenic Easements**    Scenic easements are payments to landowners to keep them from destroying everyone else's view. The original owners still own the land, but they can't spoil the scenery by putting up a three-story house on that beautiful desert mesa. Simply put, the landowner is compensated for not using the land.

**Diminished Value**    If you have ever been in an auto accident that was not your fault, and your new car was severely damaged but repairable, you probably got your car fixed. However, everyone knows that a repaired car is a previously damaged car, and does not demand the same resale value. Even though it may look and operate the same, the car is still not as desirable as the same vehicle that was never in an accident. That difference is diminished value.

**Pain and Suffering**    The value of pain and suffering usually lands in the courts, and the courts usually rely on "experts" to put a value on it. Then the protracted legal discussions begin. This is an area in which many, many issues are introduced, but suffice it to say that even something as intangible as pain can be described in dollars and cents.

**Bad Behavior**    In a book entitled *The No Asshole Rule: Building a Civilized Workplace and Surviving One That Isn't,* published in February 2007, Robert I. Sutton, a Stanford professor, gives an example of how a company may actually quantify bad behavior to get its point across. Employee Ethan's consistently bad behavior was to be calculated and deducted from his bonus, the cost of which was estimated as follows:

| | |
|---|---|
| Time spent by Ethan's direct supervisor | 250 hours valued at $25,000 |
| Time spent by HR professionals | 50 hours valued at $5,000 |
| Time spent by senior executives | 15 hours valued at $10,000 |
| Time spent by the company's outside employment counsel | 10 hours valued at $5,000 |
| Cost of recruiting and training a new secretary to support Ethan | $85,000 |
| Overtime costs associated with Ethan's last-minute demands | $25,000 |
| Anger management training and counseling | $5,000 |
| Total cost of bad behavior for the year | $160,000 |

How, then, do we value values in a nonprofit context? We do that, to borrow a Wall Street term, by voting with our checkbooks. We fund those nonprofits that exemplify, improve, and enhance those beliefs we personally hold dear. What a person is doing when he or she helps fund a nonprofit is allowing his or her values to be manifested. Nonprofit ROI as prescribed in this book does not attempt to value the values people hold dear and have a connection with, but the value of the outcomes achieved.

## THE VALUE OF EXPECTED VALUE

*Expected value* is a closely related term to ROI, and in the case of nonprofit ROI, is especially useful. It is often difficult for a nonprofit to use information after the fact, or *ex post*, to determine ROI because the information needed simply was not collected. It is then necessary to predict the outcomes that will be realized by the NPO's efforts, or *ex ante*, and apply the projected expenditures to determine an expected ROI.

Expected value brings in the added dimension of risk. Risk, according to *Webster's*, is "a hazard; a peril; exposure to loss or injury." If people decide to engage in driving while drunk, they are taking the chance that they will be arrested, or even worse, injure themselves or others. Driving drunk is risky (and stupid, irresponsible, and costly). This is not the context in which we are discussing.

If one decides to bet on who will win the Super Bowl, one is taking the chance that he or she will lose money. Betting is risky. If one decided to invest in the stock market, that investment may be lost. Investing is very risky. More appropriately, risk for the purposes of our discussion is defined as *variability of outcome.* If the outcome is not exactly known, there is an element of risk; that is, there is a variability of outcome.

Two examples will be helpful. The first deals with a popular television show, *Deal or No Deal,* to illustrate the concept of expected value. The second presents a more applicable use of expected value for a nonprofit engaged in the human services sector.

## Deal or No Deal

The popular network television show *Deal or No Deal* makes extensive use of expected value. In fact, the entire show is an exercise in applying expected value to make decisions. A contestant is first presented with 26 choices of briefcases, each of which happens to be held by a beautiful female, which has nothing whatsoever to do with the decision process. Let me rephrase that: technically, nothing whatsoever to do with the decision process. Each briefcase contains a dollar value ranging from $1 million to one penny. The contestant picks one briefcase to keep, which remains unopened, and then goes through a series of eliminations of the remaining briefcases, hoping to eliminate those containing lower dollar values.

As each chosen briefcase is opened and the amount revealed, the value of the remaining unopened briefcases will go either up or down. The value goes up when the larger amounts remain in play, and down when the smaller amounts remain in play. Throughout this process, the contestant is tempted by a mysterious entity known only as "the Banker" to accept an offer of cash in exchange for what might be contained in the contestant's chosen briefcase—prompting the all-important question: "Deal or No Deal?"

In the few times the author has viewed this program, the offer by the Banker is always less than the true expected value. For example, if five cases remain and the following values remain, the expected value is calculated as follows:

$$E(V) = \sum_{i=1}^{n} V_i \times P_i$$

Which is:

> The sum of each probability of occurrence multiplied by its possible outcome, which is, in effect, a weighted average outcome.

Which is:

> Possible Values
> $1
> $10
> $100
> $100,000
> $1,000,000

Probability that any given case will contain $1 million: out of 5 = 20%

| Probability | × | Possible Value | = | |
|---|---|---|---|---|
| .20 | | $1 | | $.20 |
| .20 | | $10 | | $2.00 |
| .20 | | $100 | | $.20.00 |
| .20 | | $20,000 | | $20,000 |
| .20 | | $1,000,000 | | $200,000 |
| | | Total | | $222,222 |

The expected value of the decision is $222,222. At that point, the contestant should be indifferent as to which choice to make: Keep the chosen briefcase or accept the offer from the Banker. However, the Banker (in my limited viewing) does not offer $222,222, or even a nice round number like $222,000. In this case, it might be something like $210,000, or even less. While we do not want to get into the psychology of the joy of gain versus pain of loss, which is certainly at play here, expected value tells us that there is a predictable value to events, and that values can be attached to outcomes, even if the outcomes are not entirely known.

## Expected Value of Cost Savings

To make this more of a realistic example for a nonprofit, let's take the example of an organization that focuses on minimizing the potential negative consequences of adolescent pregnancies. While many more aspects could be explored, the example presented is an area in which the expected value of cost savings is substantial and easy to grasp.

**Earnings Lost**   If an adolescent mother must drop out of school to care for her baby, the opportunity costs of not graduating are revealed through the earnings lost because of not having a degree. Simply using an average wage rate of $7.50/hr., the earnings impact of 17 graduates not introduced into the economy is estimated to be $357,000 per year (including multiplier effects discussed in Chapter 8). This is the amount *not* injected into the local economy because of the absence of a high school diploma or equivalent.

Annual Earnings Opportunity Costs of Graduates = $357,000

Over a 40-year working career, this amount becomes substantial. Using an inflation rate of 2 percent, over $589,000 in earnings is lost for each nongraduate. If the NPO helps only four adolescent mothers to enter the workforce per year, the impact in just the next 10 years is over $33 million.

This chapter presented several examples of nonprofit ROI. How to build on these concepts will be explored more in-depth and with more practicality in the following chapters. Eight examples of actual, real-world cases are presented in Chapter 10.

## REFERENCES

*Deal or No Deal.* Deal or No Deal TV Game Show: NBC Official Site. Accessed February 10, 2007, http://www.nbc.com/Deal_or_No_Deal/about>.

Downes, John and Jordan Elliot Goodman, eds. *Dictionary of Finance and Investment Terms*, Third Ed. (Happauge: Barron's Educational Services, 1991, p. 375).

Sutton, Robert I. *The No Asshole Rule: Building a Civilized Workplace and Surviving One That Isn't* (Warner Business Books, February 2007). From *Fast Company* (March 2007, p. 52).

# CHAPTER 6

# Introducing the Organizational Value Proposition®

## MARKET PULL

All of this work with various nonprofit groups consistently revealed that something was missing in the nonprofit tool chest. While ROI could be calculated on projects and specific programs, a metric that encompassed the broad spectrum of the value brought by a specific organization did not exist. The many groups that had heard our message at association meetings, statewide nonprofit "summits," and grantor conferences regularly called us and asked what could be done to demonstrate their total organizational value. They wanted something that would work in a variety of situations, including grant proposals, capital campaigns, and annual reports. This led us to develop something we call an Organizational Value Proposition (OVP). It had such a nice ring to it we trademarked it.

This concept is similar to Economic Value Added (EVA). In fact, the term *EVA* is a registered trademark of Stern Stewart & Company, a financial consulting firm. EVA is an estimate of true economic profit, derived from adjustments to accounting profit, with the most notable being the cost of capital. Cost of capital, which will be discussed later, is the opportunity cost of the funds used to generate the aforementioned profit.

OVP and EVA attempt to do the same thing, but in completely different arenas. EVA attempts to paint a true economic picture of the for-profit firm, and OVP attempts to paint a true economic value of the nonprofit organization. The difference is that EVA has a standardized set of inputs, accounting statements produced according to Generally Accepted Accounting Principles (GAAP), and OVP has no such standardized set of inputs, since it is based on the mission of the nonprofit. Last time we checked, there were no Generally Accepted Mission Principles, and each mission is unique in its own right.

Much of the current literature on nonprofit effectiveness also focuses on the wrong thing. This is like the old joke about economists:

> An economist, after spending considerable time in a local bar with friends, enjoying many of the various beverages they serve, was walking to his car when he realized he had lost his keys. An hour later, those he had left at the bar came out to find him standing under a streetlight looking for his missing keys. He kept looking and looking in the same relatively small area. "Why are you looking here?" his friends asked. "Your car is around the building in the parking lot." "This is where the light is," he responded.

Focusing on what is available, like Form 990 information, is simply looking where the light is, not where the answers really reside. Many watchdog groups annually evaluate nonprofits based on the percentage of their total budget going to programs versus how much is spent on fundraising. Evaluating how much is spent on fundraising is dramatically missing the point, and a disservice to the many nonprofits that operate on a smaller stage but have little public awareness. Focusing on fundraising costs as compared to the impact the funds helped accomplished is akin to focusing on outputs instead of outcomes.

## It's the Economy, Stupid! Revisited

This phrase was made popular during the Bill Clinton presidential campaign of 1992. The story goes that it was coined by Democratic strategist James Carville and hung on the wall of the Little Rock campaign headquarters to keep everyone on message. The version that would apply in this context is "It's the value, stupid!"

The journey of developing a framework to demonstrate organizational value of a nonprofit began with a phrase you have heard several times in previous chapters:

*Provide value to investors.*

The result of any sort of organizational ROI needed to incorporate the many facets of value provided by a particular NPO had to be communicated in a way the target audience understood, which is no small feat since nonprofits deal with many audiences. Typically, this means their board, large granting institutions, and the private sector, and each has very different ways of communicating. While there is danger in generalizing about these three groups, their differences and how to best communicate what they think they want are important.

## Boards

It is not unusual for a nonprofit board to be comprised of other NPO leaders, public sector people (often elected or appointed), and the private sector. This makes for an interesting mix of management styles and the issue of how to best communicate organizational value to a wide variety of board members. Even though their backgrounds and styles widely vary, the common denominator among these groups is that they operate on the policy level of the institution, not the operational level, and are most concerned with values that are easily related to their mission.

## Granting Intuitions

**Public Sector (otherwise known as the government)**  Large public sector granting institutions have very detailed and complicated grant proposal requirements. These days, most of them have a section entitled "Outcomes to Be Achieved," or similar statement. This group also plays at the level of demonstrating value that reflects the mission, and seems to be most concerned with the *intent* to produce valuable outcomes in a future program of work. If this intent is well documented and written well, this group is usually satisfied.

**Private Foundations**   While this depends on the size of the foundation, most seem to do a good job of drilling down to the next level of demonstrating value: that of specific programs. Since many private foundations have a set of defined parameters in which they will invest, they have the ability to be a better judge of effectiveness within that particular area, and are therefore more interested in program values.

## Private Sector

The private sector is at the same time more demanding and easier to please. Since they are businesspeople, they are accustomed to the vocabulary of ROI, and welcome its use. This is a territory they traverse every day. If it is a public company, at any given moment of any given day, they can determine how their company is doing by checking their respective stock price. They are judged on metrics such as market share, sales, units, margins, and profit. These are objective measures that can be calculated, verified, and reported across departments, divisions, and even countries. They are comfortable with the idea of being evaluated by numbers. They are more demanding in the sense that since they are comfortable with the concept and the calculation, the accuracy of the analysis is held to a higher level.

## OVERCOMING THE PUSHBACK

Nonprofits, as compared to for-profits, are not as comfortable with "performance measurements." In fact, the very idea of this sparks heated debate as to the appropriateness of even trying to do this, even when the reasons for doing so are numerous.

For example, there used to be a sign in most Wal-Mart stores that said, "Today's stock price is X." It may still be there, but its presence has not been noticed lately. It was there for everyone to see, including store managers, employees, and customers. And it serves many purposes:

- A benchmark of financial performance
- A metric that can be used to motivate
- What the market thinks of the future prospects of the company

- How one's retirement plan is doing, assuming investment in company stock
- A distillation of all of the information about the company into a single number

One did not have to be a stock analyst to see that a higher number was good, and a lower number was bad. One did not have to understand how to determine future cash flows, estimate the cost of capital, and present value cash flows back at the appropriate discount rate, to determine the stock price. That one number, stock price, said it all. It could be discussed and debated, bought because it was thought to be too low, or shorted because it was too high, but it was what it was. The market is always right, even if it's not correct.

Nonprofits, of course, do not have stock price. But they desire a way in which they could demonstrate their value, since if they are judged to be a provider of value, they are more likely to attract investment. This brings up a distinct difference between nonprofits and for-profits: Is money an input or an output? As Jim Collins states so well in his monograph *Good to Great and the Social Sectors*, "This distinction between inputs and outputs is fundamental, yet frequently missed."

The answer to the original question, "Is money an input or an output?" is "It depends." The author admits that this is a classic economist's response, and apologizes for it. In the for-profit world, money is obviously an input, and takes many forms such as seed capital, initial public offerings, venture capital, debt, common stock offerings, and so on. It is also an output, and as discussed previously, is comprehensively manifested in stock price.

One invests in stocks so one can make a profit when that stock is sold. The same can be said for inventory, real estate, commodities, or even works of art. To be clear, there may be other reasons why one may invest in these things, such as creative appreciation or the ability to take a stroll across one's own pasture, but the financial reason is the profit motive.

But is it an input or output for nonprofits? According to Jim Collins,

> The confusion between inputs and outputs stems from one of the primary differences between business and the social sectors. In business, money is both an input (a resource for achieving greatness) and an output (a measure of greatness). In the social sectors, money is only an input, and not a measure of greatness.

This author could not agree more. A nonprofit should not be judged by how much money it accumulates, but by how it fulfills its mission. A more financially based version of this same thought is that a nonprofit should achieve maximum impact, relative to its mission and its resources. A cornerstone of this book is that the demonstration of that impact, of *fulfilling its mission relative to its resources*, uses financial methodologies to describe the value of the outputs of nonprofits, and sometimes that can be misinterpreted. The values of the outcomes produced by the NPO are often described in dollars, and that is not the same as defining money as an output in the context of inputs and outputs.

## STRUCTURAL OBSTACLES

The original intention of an Organizational Value Proposition was to somehow replicate the distillation of as much information as possible into a comprehensive, understandable, and useful set of metrics, much as stock price in an efficient capital market reflects all information, both public and private. There are several "structural" reasons why this is an extremely difficult endeavor:

### No Common Denominator

As previously mentioned, money is an output in the private sector, and money is money. We all use the same currency, at least in this country, and all know that a dollar is a dollar. Money, usually in the form of profits, is also the numerator in almost any "return" ratio, such as return on invested capital, return on assets, return on sales, and so on. Nonprofits have no such common denominator to be derived from accounting statements. If success in the nonprofit arena is defined as fulfilling one's mission relative to its resources, with the myriad missions it's easy to see how difficult comparisons can be.

### No Rational Capital Market

The private sector has developed a mechanism that channels resources to those firms that it feels will provide the most return relative to the risk taken:

the capital market. This capital market functions as a clearinghouse of information that is ultimately reflected in the financial instruments, stock and bonds, of a given company. An assumption of many economic theories is that capital markets, or more appropriately the participants in those markets, act in a rational way. Defining *rational* is itself a challenge, but for the purposes of this discussion, let's define it as acting in a way that maximizes one's satisfaction. Satisfaction in the context of a capital market participant is profit or an acceptable return on investment.

If an investment is projected to provide an acceptable level of return, or more return than is warranted by the risk, capital will flow to that company. In other words, success will attract more money. Conversely, failing to provide an acceptable level of return will cause capital to flow away from that particular company. The faster and cheaper this flow takes place, the more efficiently the market is operating.

The nonprofit arena does not have this clearing house in which funding is bought and sold. There is no mechanism where supply and demand meet at a given price and quantity and the market is judged to be in equilibrium. There is no efficient market where information is accessible to all at no cost, all participants know what to do with that information, and ultimately channel their money to those opportunities where inefficiencies can be exploited at a profit.

When a nonprofit does a good job of fulfilling its mission relative to its resources, more funding may flow to it, or may not. If the NPO does well at publicizing its success, leverages early funding into a more expansive capital campaign, and gets the right people involved who prompt others to invest, then more funding may follow, but it certainly cannot be described as a market in a strict economic sense, and certainly not as an efficient market.

In this case, if the pool of all potential nonprofit funders can be viewed as a market, then there is evidence that money flows to the biggest fish in the pond. The *Chronicle of Philanthropy* reported that in 2005 the biggest 400 charities accounted for $1 out of every $4 raised by all charities, and that giving was up 13 percent for that same group for the year. *Giving USA*, the annual report published by the Giving USA Foundation, states that giving overall grew at only 2.7 percent for the same period. The question becomes why this is the case. Is it because they are providing the highest return on investment, even if esoterically defined, or is it because they have the biggest fundraising machine operating at full throttle?

## No Universally Accepted Reporting Standards

Many nonprofits report their financial information according to the pronouncements of the Financial Accounting Standards Board (FASB). The problem is that these standards do not always provide a consistent picture with information required for an IRS Form 990. The fact that colleges and universities are not required to complete a Form 990, for instance, makes comparisons even more difficult.

Many reports are now published by watchdog groups on nonprofit activity, and more of these groups seem to pop up every time a new scandal breaks. Unfortunately, many of these reports focus on how much is spent on fundraising compared to how much is spent on programs. This approach is misguided because their analysis is based on information reported on Form 990. A good accountant can take the same information and present it several ways, depending on timing, allocation, and even job descriptions. Fundraising expenses are reported, but are subject to many interpretations, many of which are equally legal and appropriate.

## No Standard Feedback Mechanisms

Pierre Omidyar is a name with which those in Silicon Valley, venture capitalists, and buyers and sellers of things found in one's attic will be familiar. He is the founder of eBay, by many measures the most successful company of the dot-com era. In 1999, with billions made from eBay, he started his charitable foundation to help nonprofits. In 2004, he basically shut the foundation down and launched Omidyar Network to fund both nonprofits and for-profits.

When asked by *Fast Company* magazine what were ". . . the constraints of the nonprofit sector that pushed you to start investing in for-profit organizations?" this was the response:

> One was the lack of good feedback mechanisms. How does a nonprofit know when it's doing well? If the nonprofit is not making progress and it's running out of money, the message becomes, "Our work is not yet done, and we need more capital." Whereas in the business world, you have lots of feedback mechanisms, including the discipline of the bottom line.

Couldn't have said it better myself. Nonprofits have used the convenient excuse of not having enough money to fulfill their mission, so therefore no results yet, for years.

# Intended Uses

While a single metric such as stock price may not exist for a nonprofit world, the message we heard over and over was the need for a comprehensive set of numbers that could be used in a various contexts. The most common were:

## Strategic Planning

Like their for-profit counterparts, nonprofits spend a lot of organizational resources on strategic planning, possibly even more so. This is because NPOs often get paid, in effect, to take the time to do the planning via planning grants. Planning grants are just what the name implies: funding to write a business plan, per se, for a nonprofit. Those who have served on nonprofit boards have in many instances been trained to associate strategic planning with the requisite annual board retreat, with it often not being a fond association due to the amount of time it consumed.

Value metrics in a strategic planning context allow decisions to be based on the value of the outcomes produced, which brings in a large dose of objectivity into the process. This is similar to capital budgeting in the private sector, where a project is judged on the present value of future cash flow, discounted at the firm's weighted average cost of capital.

## Reporting Context

An important part of the investment-driven model discussed in Chapter 4 is that investors need to be treated as investors. Proof of fully adopting this is an active investor relations effort. If funders are brought into the organization under the investment-driven umbrella, they deserve to be kept informed as to how their investment is performing.

The reasoning here is no different from people putting money into their IRA or 401 (k), and checking their balance online, usually after the kids go to bed and things have quieted down. It's unlikely that any action will be taken; one just wants to know how things are going. Investors in NPO feel the same way: They just want to know how things are going.

Not only is this important for previous investors; it's also important that this reporting is in place to attract future investors.

## Funding Context

Perhaps the most important of all uses was the ability to demonstrate the value in a funding context. As Robert J. Ringer said in his 1977 book *Looking Out for #1*, "... the best way to help the poor is by not becoming one of them." Sometimes nonprofits had grant writing in mind; other times it was for a capital campaign, and still other times it was part of a sustainability plan.

From a fundraising perspective, an OVP is the Swiss Army Knife in the nonprofit fundraising toolbox. It has many uses, some of which have yet to be discovered. What they all share is that they attempt to answer, to the best of their ability, "What's in it for me?" Ultimately, what they must do is demonstrate value to investors.

## ◼ REFERENCES

Breen, Bill. "Pierre Omidyar's Network Funds Both Nonprofits and For-Profits: No Matter, as Long as They Do Good." *Fast Company* (March 2007, p. 90).

Clinton, Bill. http://en.wikipedia.org/wiki/It's_the_economy,_stupid 2/18/2007.

Collins, Jim. *Good to Great and the Social Sector: A Monograph to Accompany Good to Great* (Boulder: Jim Collins, 2005).

Barton, Noelle and Holly Hall. "Special Report: A Year of Big Gains." *Chronicle of Philanthropy: The Newspaper of the Nonprofit World* (October 26, 2006).

Omidyar, Pierre. *Lessons Learned from Pam and Pierre.* Accessed March 1 2007, http://www.givingspace.org/omidyar.htm.

Ringer, Robert J. *Looking Out for #1* (New York: Fawcett Crest Books, 1977).

# PART TWO

# ROI Foundations
# and Techniques

# Building an OVP® for your Organization

One of the sayings we have repeated for years is, "We can torture any number until it confesses." While perhaps a bit harsh sounding, the point that almost any nonprofit-related situation can be described by numbers and improved by ROI is true.

What follows in this chapter are the most common ways we have found to demonstrate value, but they are by no means the only ways. Sometimes, the method must rely on more qualitative measures, where a story is being built, a picture is being painted, or a lawyer is assembling evidence. Sometimes, the evidence is circumstantial, but if that's all one has, the case still has to be built.

At the other end of the spectrum, we have quantitative methods, where the lawyer can build the case on hard evidence, the scientist can run the experiment, or the mathematician can present the proof. We have found that this type of demonstration is more compelling than the purely qualitative approach.

# FIVE STEPS TO DEMONSTRATING VALUE

In today's culture of 30 second sound bites and 15 minutes of fame, we learned long ago to employ Occam's razor. No, this is not a middle-eastern brand of shaving apparatus, but a principle attributed to a 14th-century Franciscan friar William of Ockham. Occam's razor puts forth that extraneous and unnecessary assumptions should be "shaved off," thereby resulting in a simpler and more correct solution.

The Latin *entia non sunt multiplicanda praeter necessitatem* loosely translates to:

*All things being equal, the simplest solution tends to be the best one.*

This is one reason why a correctly crafted OVP seems to work with today's funders. They want to see the value of their investment in terms they understand and appreciate, and the easier it is for them to connect the dots, the more satisfied they become.

While every OVP is by nature going to be different, the general steps in crafting one are the same:

1. *Determine* the motivations of your stakeholders.
2. *Develop* a program with definable outcomes.
3. *Translate* outcomes into specific benefits.
4. *Demonstrate* effectiveness in investment terms.
5. *Report* results on a regular basis.

## 1. Determine the Motivations of Your Stakeholders

Sound impossible? Until these motivations are uncovered, a value proposition cannot be crafted. Still, these motivations are often assumed. The chorus of excuses goes something like this:

- I have too many stakeholders to be expected to know what their motivations are!
- Motivations for what?
- I don't have the time to do that.
- Even if I had the time, I don't know how to do something like that.
- Surveys are not my strong suit.

The only way to determine stakeholder motivations is deceivingly simple:

*Ask them!*

What and whom does one ask? (in question-and-answer format)

- With which stakeholders are we most concerned? *Your primary funders.*
- What type of survey instrument do I use? *A private conversation.*
- What do I ask them? *What they feel are the organization's primary outcomes.*
- Put differently, ex post: *Why did they invest in your organization?*
- Put differently, ex ante: *Why would they invest in your organization?*
- *Or, What do they need to see as an outcome in order to invest?*

The range of responses will probably not be as varied or earth shattering as one may think. In fact, stakeholders are normally champing at the bit to let their expectations be known!

## 2. Develop a Program with Definable Outcomes

This is the point at which the difference between outcomes and outputs becomes extremely obvious. As a refresher, outputs are defined as the tangible results of a process or program. Outcomes are broadly defined as the impacts the organization wants to have on people or society. Potential investors want to see what they are investing in, plain and simple. If an organization cannot define what they will do with the money, they certainly do not have the credibility to deliver on any outcomes promised.

Being able to define outcomes can be trickier than it may seem. Part of the reason may be that the NPO does not have the tools or skills to do it. But, as illustrated in the following examples, it is more likely the result of human nature.

**Example: Economic Development**  Economic development organizations often fly below the radar in terms of public familiarity with them being a nonprofit. However, almost every county and city of any size in this country has at least one such entity. They can be Chambers of Commerce, Economic Development Commissions, Economic Development Councils, Industrial Development Boards, or departments within a city or county government.

Most of them, somewhere in their mission statement, employ versions of the phrases "create jobs," "increase wage levels," and "improve the local economy." For years, our work with them has been to direct them through the process to define a reasonable job goal for the program on which they are raising money. We can then take that job goal and produce some great values that really get their target prospect's attention. A weighted average wage of their targeted industries is developed, and then industry-specific multipliers are applied. The result is a gross estimate of dollars that will be generated in the area if their job goals materialize. This bottom-up process of building up to a gross impact is then broken down into how it will likely be spent in the local economy. This is why targeted prospects, who are usually local businesspeople, like this process so much: It answers the "What's in it for me?" question as directly as possible. An actual example of this model appears in Chapter 10.

The most difficult step in the entire process is to get an organization to agree to a job goal. While it might be human nature to not want to be held to a number that can be affected by so many outside influences, the very effective process described previously cannot be completed unless this early step is completed. Organizations and their executives are reluctant to be pinned down on a job goal number, and the comments we hear, such as those here, signify their level of anxiousness:

- What if we don't reach it?
- Why stick my neck out on something that is so dependent on the national economy?
- Too many things affect this that are beyond my control.

The points that are missed in this are that:

1. It is a projection, not a promise.
2. It is not etched in granite. Projections can, and should, change.
3. If one wants the "armor-piercing ammunition" of the value to the local businesses, one has to have a place to start.

It is difficult to raise money for a program unless the values of the outcomes are demonstrated.

**Example: Education/Social Services**    A good example of the reluctance to be pinned down on an outcome often appears in those cases where the results cannot be measured for a number of years and incur a significant cost to track. For an example, we will use the educational program from Chapter 5 that provided classes for 200 people to get their GED certificate. The goal in that case was to have a 50 percent pass rate, or 100 people earning a GED. A far better goal was to ensure 80 of these graduates become employed. It was easy to measure how many passed the test. These results would be immediately determined. The goal of 80 of these graduates becoming employed would take some time.

Again, the reluctance to go to this level is heard:

- Our job is to educate them, not get them a job.
- We are not an employment agency.
- They also need job search skills, and that is beyond our scope.
- We do not have the budget to do that.

Yes, these reasons are technically correct. And, with outlooks like this, it is not surprising that it is difficult to get outside funders interested. For a moment, put yourself in the place of a potential outside funder who is being asked to invest in this program:

- He or she realizes that education is important to improve one's quality of life.
- He or she understands that it is easier to get a job if one has a high school diploma.
- He or she knows that a person is likely to earn more with a high school diploma.

This anecdotal evidence may get the organization some small level of financial support. Think of how that support could be increased if the organization could demonstrate the value of these outcomes in general:

- Eighty of these graduates will have better job skills.
- The available labor pool will be increased.
- On-the-job training time will be reduced because of a better skill at entry.

Taking these outcomes to the next level by translating them into specific benefits is the next step.

## 3. Translate Outcomes into Specific Benefits

The first step in the translation process is determining the intended audience. It can radically change how an ROI presentation is crafted. Are they qualitative people or quantitative people? Are they emotionally motivated or "What's in it for me?" people. Do they have "skin in the game" or are they just the type who are openly opinionated and want everyone else to know what they think?

**Primary vs. Supporting Customers**    This distinction was first introduced to us through the Drucker Foundation's Self Assessment Tool, written by management guru Peter F. Drucker. Drucker is credited with many things, among them the early identification and increasing importance of knowledge workers. He authored some 20+ books and other publications in his lifetime, and in 1990 founded the Peter F. Drucker Foundation for Nonprofit Management, now the Leader to Leader Institute.

As defined by Drucker, a *primary customer* "is the person whose life is changed through your work." *Supporting customers* "are volunteers, members, partners, funders, referral sources, employees, and others who must be satisfied." This distinction is important, since if one is to translate outcomes into benefits, what the intended audience values must be determined.

In the context of this book, our focus is the supporting customer. These are the people who fund the organization. Drucker asks, "Who must be satisfied for the organization to achieve results?" The answer is, of course, *all customers*. An allegory of this statement, as it has been stated rather harshly in the nonprofit sector for years, is "No margin, no mission." In other words, no matter how well the primary customer is served, without supporting customers, the organization will not exist.

Closely related to this distinction of primary and supporting customers is the question of "What does our customer value?" Primary customers, since they are the primary recipients of the service or product provided by the nonprofit, will have a completely different set of criteria to define value, compared to a supporting customer. Exhibit 7.1, using a hypothetical example of a homeless shelter that provides a safe place to sleep and a hot meal, shows that the differences can be dramatic.

**Relative vs. Absolute Value**    The word *value* itself can be further broken down into relative or absolute value. Relative value is most appropriate when

EXHIBIT 7.1    **THE DIFFERENCE IN WHAT IS VALUED**

| Primary Customer Examples | Supporting Customer Examples |
|---|---|
| Easy to find | An appropriate number assisted |
| Open at appropriate times | Operating within the budget |
| Clean | Using resources effectively |
| Safe | An organization to be proud of |
| Feels like home | Improving the community |
| A trusting environment | Making a difference |
| Friendly people | Filling a need in the community |
| A safe haven | Helping those less fortunate |

the potential investor is looking for a reason to invest in one nonprofit over another. Absolute value is more appropriate when the credibility of the NPO is the critical factor. The differences in how the value proposition is constructed are important.

*The Relative Value for a Bank Manager*    Banks seem to always be on the hit list of nonprofits looking for money, and banks have trained the nonprofit community well. They always seem to find a way to give something, even if a small amount. They are some of the best of corporate citizens.

Is this because they just have so much money to give? Is it that every community has at least one? Or is it because they understand the benefit of supporting the community from a self-interest perspective; almost everyone is a customer in one way or another. Whatever one may believe, banks always have a long list of nonprofits wanting money, and must decide how to disperse their funding.

One of the decision processes banks use is comparing the relative merits of each request. They ostensibly try their best to spread their funding around effectively, to honor as many requests as possible. The conversation usually goes something like this:

> I like the (insert nonprofit name here). In fact, one of our employee's children gets treatment there. I think you do good work for our community. Our philanthropic budget is $200,000, and it's all spoken for this year. But I want to help, so here's what I'll do. I'll borrow (no pun intended) from next year's budget. I can get you a check for $10,000 as soon as our new fiscal year starts in July.

The decision framework in this case is that the bank is deciding *between* nonprofits, so as long as your organization is perceived to be more effective in fulfilling its mission, and the mission is deemed important to the local bank, the request is responded to positively.

**The Absolute Value for a Wealthy Retiree**   In this example, the prospect is not deciding between NPOs, but on the amount to give to a specific organization. In this case, the decision of how much to invest in the organization relies on many points, including:

- Their level of motivation
- The quality of the *ask*
- The credibility of the organization
- The capacity of the prospect

Experience has shown that at this stage in the process, when the prospect is considering not whether to invest, but how much to invest, the absolute level of the investment hinges on the credibility of the organization. At the end of the day, the investor wants to know that his or her investment is going to make a difference in a prudently managed way.

**Back to the GED**   Let's get back to the example first introduced in Step 2, the educational program for 200 people to get their GED. We talked previously of how defining the outcomes appropriately will help in the demonstration of value. Let's drill one level deeper in the defining of these outcomes, and explore how translating these outcomes into specific benefits can be so powerful.

Moving from a general description of how a GED can benefit an area to a more personal example, think of how support could be increased even more if the organization could demonstrate the value of these outcomes to a specific business or industry—in this case, what it would mean to a local grocery store owner:

- Eighty additional graduates will add $960,000 in direct earnings per year to the local economy.
- This $960,000 per year has an impact of over $1.7 million per year.
- An additional $120,000 per year will be spent in local grocery stores.

Again, at this stage in the process, the question of "What's in it for me?" has been addressed. The question now becomes whether the organization can deliver on what it is promising.

## 4. Demonstrate Effectiveness in Investment Terms

One cannot expect an outside investor to believe an organization has adopted the investment-driven model if the organization continues to use the terms *donation* or *gift*. The terminology used must reflect the vernacular of the situation. Exhibit 7.2 presents a list of terms and methodologies that have proven to be the most effective.

Adopting this type of language signals three things:

1.  *The organization did its homework.* Rather than just talk a good game, using this type of vocabulary demonstrates that the NPO took the time to collect meaningful data, analyze it, interpret it, and present it in a meaningful way. This is head and shoulders above an anecdotal story, purely emotional appeal, or arm-twisting. It shows that the organization can objectively prove that it has impact.

2.  *They have moved beyond the anecdotal.* While anecdotal stories and examples have their place, moving beyond them raises the level of sophistication of the message and demonstrates that the NPO is being accountable and transparent. It also reinforces the concept of being other-centered, rather than organization-centered, by using the language of the prospect, not the language of the organization.

3.  *They have successfully differentiated themselves from other nonprofits.* Presenting the message in investment terms significantly differentiates an NPO from the rest of the crowd. While many NPOs now claim that they are delivering ROI, in fact they are just using a popular term and presenting outputs at best.

## EXHIBIT 7.2    EFFECTIVE INVESTMENT TERMS

- Net present value
- Per-capita improvement
- Payback period
- Social impact per dollar invested
- Return per dollar spent
- Local economic impact
- Business-to-business impacts

## 5. Report Results on a Regular Basis

Investors want to be kept informed. It is as simple as that. On a personal level, our instant information-based society has trained us well. When the stock market is having an extremely good or bad day, those who are invested in the stock market through their 401(k), IRA, or private account click on their portfolio value repeatedly, second only to the Final Four basketball office pool. It's human nature that when something very personal (your money) is given over to someone else (a nonprofit) for stewardship, a natural curiosity regularly surfaces to want to know how it is performing.

Again borrowing from the corporate world, we term this category of effort "investor relations." Many fundraisers have adopted this language and purport to be able to do this for NPOs on a consulting basis, but we have found that the nonprofits themselves do a much better job of it. There are many ways to keep investors informed, from e-newsletters to campaign brochures to annual reports. They need not be professionally designed or expensively printed, but if an organization is to truly adopt the investment-driven model, they need to treat investors as investors. Three inventive examples of how actual clients have done this are presented in Chapter 9.

## AREAS OF FOCUS

While every value proposition is unique, over the years they have fallen into some common categories. All of the following are actual examples of nonprofit OVPs, with the names of the organizations all changed to the *Center* to protect the confidentiality of the client. Most OVPs would incorporate four or five of the following areas.

### 1. The Value of the Organization as an Entity

This component finds its way into almost every OVP. It presents the impact of the organization itself, just as any other going concern. This component represents the impact of the organization's payroll, employment, and spending. No programmatic values are included in this section, which presents the most powerful message when the organization has many employees or a large budget but can be used no matter how large the organization. An actual example follows:

**Example: Entity Impact**    The Center impacts the area just as any other business entity that employs people and purchases goods and services. Each dollar paid in earnings to the Center employees is spent for living expenses, rent, food, and so on, at businesses who also have employees, who then spend their earnings on other goods and services, and so on. This is often referred to as the *ripple effect*.

The following impacts, which only reflect the hard dollars expended, may underestimate the true value of the services provided by the Center. Using only current budget data, the Center as an organization has the following *annual* impacts:

*Earnings Impact*    As the wages paid by the Center are circulated throughout the area, their impact becomes substantially larger. Current administrative costs of $285,817 per year are estimated to have a *$502,303 annual* earnings impact. In other words, each dollar the Center pays in salary causes another $.76 in earnings to be generated in the community.

*Employment Impact*    Each job at the Center has the effect of influencing the need for other jobs at area businesses. The Center's full-time equivalent of 4.25 people is estimated to stimulate the need for 1.96 additional jobs in the area.

*Overall Economic Impact*    The total expenditures of the Center can    also be used to estimate their total economic impact. Current spending of $ 957,105 per year is estimated to create *$1,539,041 worth of commerce* (final demand) in the area.

## 2. Service Delivery Values

Most nonprofits provide some sort of service rather than product, and these services range from making loans to teaching specific skills to providing an otherwise unavailable experience. Because of this very broad spectrum, no particular methodology or model is more common than any other. What is common to all of these is that NPOs usually deliver these services on a very cost-effective basis compared to the private sector. (We will skip the theoretical issues on whether nonprofits really compete with the private sector, or the fact that by some definitions they operate in a sector in which for-profit firms cannot earn a profit.) In other words, they do a lot with a little.

Here are two examples of how service delivery values have been illustrated.

**Example A: Health Services Delivery**   The Center serves the area in many ways, the most notable being Family Practice, Dental Practice, Outreach, Child Care, and Pharmacy areas. Over 3,700 people use the services of the Center annually. Rather than just report the number of people who receive medical assistance, counseling on health issues, daycare, and so on, which are measures of output, this report focuses on outcomes whenever possible. Each functional area of the organization has unique characteristics that allow for more specific, and accurate, impacts to be presented. The family practice area is presented in Exhibit 7.3.

This organization treats over 3,100 people per year at a total cost slightly over $255 per person; this is even more impressive when the fact that the population served is much more likely to be uninsured and, therefore, relatively further progressed in their particular affliction.

**Example B: Rural Loan Program**   The Center serves as a catalyst to provide the funding necessary to build facilities, purchase needed equipment, and implement new technology. Rather than just report the number

**EXHIBIT 7.3    FAMILY PRACTICE VALUE**

| | |
|---|---:|
| Input characteristics | |
| Number of annual encounters | 8,828 |
| Number of annual users | 3,183 |
| Full-time equivalent employment | 4.41 |
| Total payroll expenditures | $558,500 |
| Total annual cost (including overhead allocation) | $812,612 |
| Area economic impacts | |
| Total economic impact | $1,159,760 |
| Employment impact | 6.7 |
| Earnings impact | $698,069 |
| Community return ratios | |
| Additional dollars returned per dollar invested | 1.43 |
| Additional jobs created per job | 1.51 |
| Additional earnings created per dollar paid | 1.25 |
| Community economic value | |
| Actual economic value of service provided per person served (based on increase in final demand of other businesses; does not include indirect benefits such as prevention) | $364 |

of loans made or the total amount loaned, which are measures of output, this report focuses on the outcomes of those efforts.

Each type of loan was analyzed based on how the proceeds of the loans were used. The analysis uses information on the 25 loans made over a 4½-year period. Actual loan amounts are kept confidential. Loan proceeds were treated as follows:

> Facility loans = increase in capital investment
>
> Equipment = increase in equipment spending
>
> Technology loans = increase in computer/technology spending

This classification of loans by functional area allows for more specific, and accurate, impacts to be presented.

Most of these loans include local bank participation. Even if bank participation is excluded from the analysis, the impact attributable to the Center's funds alone is $6,616,619.

| | |
|---|---|
| Number of loans in analysis | 25 |
| Total technology loan impact | $ 1.2 million |
| Total equipment loan impact | $ 1.7 million |
| Total facility loan impact | $17.0 million |
| Overall loan impact | $19.9 million |

## 3. Social Outcomes Enhanced

The ubiquitous *good work* that is supplied and created by nonprofits is prevalent in almost every niche of society. In our experience, education, health, and economic development are the most popular areas in which enhanced outcomes can be demonstrated, but almost every nonprofit produces some outcome that produces more impact as time goes on. The two examples presented are from a housing assistance program for the working poor and a medical care program for the uninsured/underinsured.

**Example A: Housing Assistance**   The Center produces outcomes that help the entire community by helping create 270 new homeowners per year. Through its educational classes and assistance in securing loans, the benefits of home equity, more disposable income, and neighborhood revitalization produce bottom-line effects.

*Home Equity Created*   A home is the largest purchase made by the average American. It creates wealth by appreciating faster than inflation, while the cost remains fixed. While appreciation varies widely by neighborhood and region, a conservative rate of 3 percent, adjusted for inflation, is included in this analysis.

The 270 homeowners assisted by the Center, if they hold the home for 10 years, create $20,680,029 in equity, or *$2,068,003* per year.

*Greater Income Created*   The tax laws of the United States, as they pertain to the deductibility of home mortgage interest, are considered by many to be a fundamental component of our consumer-driven economy. Again, using the 270 homeowners assisted by the Center, the income is "created" by not having to be paid in taxes. This additional income is akin to a tax cut from an economic stimulus perspective.

| | |
|---|---:|
| Average first year of interest | $36, 448, 650 |
| × effective tax rate on $35, 057 Married Filing Jointly | 13% |
| = addition spendable income created | **$4, 738, 325** |

*Revitalization Effects*   Much evidence exists that neighborhood housing improvement is the primary driver of revitalization. This "revitalization effect" includes:

- Substantial increases in the value of the developed property itself
- Reduced municipal monitoring costs (police, fire)
- Enhanced neighborhood tax base
- Increases in surrounding neighborhood property values
- More neighborhood stability

Using a conservative figure of 10 percent appreciation applied to the $33.9 million market value of the rental units created and treating it as an increase in economic activity in the real estate industry alone, the "revitalization impact" on the local economy is over *$4,396,830* per year.

**Example B: Healthier Communities**   The Center is heavily involved in prevention, which can have large, but often indirect, impacts in future years. While few will argue the benefit prevention *can* provide, this example

| EXHIBIT 7.4 | HIGHER EARNING POSSIBLE |
|---|---|
| Average weekly wage (2000 county average) | $440 |
| Annual average wage | $22,880 |
| Number of medical users | 3,183 |
| Less number under 15 years old | 700 |
| Total adult medical users | 2,483 |
| Participation rate in labor force (2000 Georgia) | 66.1% |
| Total adult medical users in labor force | 1,641 |
| Low estimate of increased earnings due to health care access | $4,993,906 |
| High estimate of increased earnings due to health care access | $7,697,374 |

focuses on areas that pass the "test of reasonableness." In other words, in the example presented next, it is reasonable to assume that the efforts of the Center have significant, but not necessarily exclusive, influence on the positive outcomes. The area of focus in Exhibit 7.4 makes use of a respected study that reported those with access to health care had earnings that averaged 13.3 to 20.5 percent higher than those who did not have access to health care.

## 4. Societal Costs Avoided

The nonprofits involved in health and education are the natural areas to demonstrate societal savings. The calculus of societal costs avoided typically results in very large values. For example, prevention of a single case of disease can have a profound impact. Even early detection of an incurable disease can produce substantial savings to society, not to mention the quality of life enhancements to the patient.

**Example A: Health Cost Savings Due to Prevention**    In this example, the Center sought to demonstrate that access to health care could reduce preventable stays in the hospital, since early detection and treatment would cause the emergency room to be used less often as source of treatment of last resort. Exhibit 7.5 uses a study that found a 3.9 percent reduction in preventable stays when the uninsured had access to preventative medical care.

**Example B: Local Housing Cost Savings**
*Costs of Foreclosures*    The costs of foreclosure fall into two major categories: equity lost by the owner, and costs incurred by the lenders. The total cost of

EXHIBIT 7.5    **HOSPITAL STAYS PREVENTED**

| | |
|---|---|
| Number of medical users | 3,183 |
| Less number under 15 years old | 700 |
| Total adult medical users | 2,483 |
| Less number insured | 1,291 |
| Total adults uninsured | 1,192 |
| Increase in uninsureds' preventable stay days | 46 |
| Average cost savings per stay of uninsured (2002) | $3,300 |
| Total value of reduction in preventable stays | $153,374 |

foreclosures can often exceed 25 percent of the market value of the home. Since foreclosures are often predictable by the owners, increased repair and maintenance costs are also common on foreclosed homes. The Center substantially reduces these costs through its intervention and counseling programs. Annually, the Center helps prevent 297 foreclosures at an average of $36,587 each, saving lenders $8,493,658 and homeowners $2,372,682 in lost equity, for a total savings of *$10,866,337*.

*Reduced Homelessness*   The Center helps alleviate the homeless problem through self-sufficiency counseling and providing emergency shelter. In the period from 2000 to 2003, the Center provided an average of 2,741 nights of shelter annually, at a cost of $50,992 per year.

Fourteen homeless families have worked through the Center's housing continuum to become homeowners. The value of this transformation is included in the housing impacts contained in this report. The money saved by society for hospitalization, jail, and emergency shelter alone is estimated to be $24,961 per person, for a total savings of $349,454.

Seventy homeless families have also made it to self-sufficiency status. This saves an additional $1,747,270 that the public sector or philanthropic agencies would otherwise have to provide.

If just 10 persons per year are saved from being homeless by the Center, whether through counseling to become homeowners or emergency assistance, *$249,610* per year are saved by the community.

*Lower Occurrence of Crime*   Personal property crime is 52 percent more likely to occur in rental units than in a personally owned housing unit (207 occurrences per 1,000 renters compared to 136 occurrences per 1,000 homeowners). The cost per crime, in 2003 dollars, averages $1,969. Applying these numbers to the 270 new homeowners, who would otherwise have been renters, 56 of them would likely be a victim of personal property crime. The new homeowners created by the services of the Center result in a reduced crime value of *$110,264*.

***Reduced Predatory Lending*** Because many of the Center's customers earn lower incomes, they are especially vulnerable to predatory lending practices. The counseling provided by the Center virtually eliminates this possibility.

The consequences of predatory lending appear as lost equity to the homeowner, back-end penalties for early prepayment, and excess interest paid. Of the 2,648 people in 2003 counseled by the Center on home buyer education, if only 1 out of 4 are spared the cost of predatory lending, substantial savings are achieved.

662 Homeowners × $14,139 = *$9,360,018*

## 5. Local Business Impacts

The author first introduced program impacts at the local business level into a funding campaign in 1994. It was an economic development campaign, and up to that point, a generic "What 100 jobs will mean to your community," was used. The generic example was useful in demonstrating a critical point: The program that prospects were being asked to fund had demonstrable outcomes that may not be obvious at first glance. The shortcomings of the generic example, as voiced by actual funding prospects, were that:

- Our community is different.
- I don't trust the source.
- The data on which the example was based was outdated.
- It did not tell me enough to merit my investment.
- It did not answer, "What's in it for me?"

Area-specific, customized, and detailed local business impacts were the solution. An example of how this looks for an economic development campaign, where the outcome of the program was jobs, and the value of the program was how the earnings from these jobs filtered out to the local community, is presented in Exhibit 7.6.

**EXHIBIT 7.6    LOCAL COMMUNITY IMPACTS: HOW THE EARNINGS WILL LIKELY BE SPENT BASED ON EARNINGS LEVEL OF JOBS CREATED**

| | |
|---|---|
| Projected consumer expenditures | $36,936,730 |
| Expected income range of primary jobs | $30,000 to $39,999 |
| Weighted average annual wage | $31,820 |
| **Area Expenditures** | |
| **Food** | $5,308,832 |
| Food at home | $3,106,673 |
| Cereals and bakery products | $477,152 |
| Meats, poultry, fish, eggs | $832,941 |
| Dairy products | $350,603 |
| Fruits and vegetables | $526,941 |
| Other food at home | $919,036 |
| Food away from home | $2,201,122 |
| **Alcoholic beverages** | $386,908 |
| **Housing** | $11,529,438 |
| Shelter | $6,806,673 |
| Owned dwellings | $3,874,265 |
| Rented dwellings | $2,624,334 |
| Other lodging | $308,074 |
| Utilities, fuels, and public service | $2,535,128 |
| Household operations | $427,362 |
| Housekeeping supplies | $486,487 |
| Household furnishings and equipment | $1,273,788 |
| **Apparel and services** | $1,748,865 |
| **Transportation** | $7,575,302 |
| Vehicle purchases | $3,506,028 |
| Gasoline and motor oil | $1,389,964 |
| Other vehicle expenses | $2,305,888 |
| Public transportation | $373,423 |
| **Health care** | $2,050,715 |
| **Entertainment** | $1,719,821 |
| **Personal care products and services** | $541,463 |
| **Reading** | $143,146 |
| **Education** | $453,294 |
| **Tobacco products** | $370,311 |
| **Cash contributions** | $833,978 |
| **Miscellaneous** | $1,166,947 |
| **Personal insurance and pensions** | $3,111,859 |
| Life and personal insurance | $367,199 |
| Pensions and Social Security | $2,743,622 |
| **Total** | **$36,940,879** |

| EXHIBIT 7.7 | ORGANIZATIONAL VALUE PROPOSITION®: SUMMARY OF ANNUAL CENTER IMPACTS |

The value of the Center to the community can best be illustrated by an Organizational Value Proposition—a single term that summarizes the various effects of the Center's presence. These include the cost savings to society, new home construction, financing effects, and the operation of the organization itself. Using the methodology and effects previously presented, the following represents a conservative annual value of the Center to the area. Put another way, this chart illustrates the value that would be lost if the Center did not exist.

|  | Annual Impact |
|---|---|
| **Organization impacts** | |
| Total output impact | $5,212,369 |
| **Area economic benefits** | |
| Household spending | $5,232,117 |
| Property tax revenue | $491,865 |
| **Local business benefits** | |
| Lender revenue impact | $2,334,174 |
| Transaction revenue impact | $4,727,390 |
| Construction impacts | |
| Additional rental units | $1,412,160 |
| Additional development units | $5,173,510 |
| New home purchases | $3,086,627 |
| **Societal costs avoided** | |
| Foreclosure costs | $10,866,337 |
| Reduced homelessness | $249,610 |
| Lower crime costs | $110,264 |
| Reduced predatory lending | $9,360,018 |
| **Societal outcomes enhanced** | |
| Home equity created | $2,068,003 |
| Greater income created | $4,738,325 |
| Revitalization effects | $4,396,830 |
| **Total Annual Impact** | $59,459,599 |

# 6. Overall Economic Impact

*Economic impact* is one of the most overused terms in today's popular press. The reporting of any major event in any major city carries an economic impact number, usually in the hundreds of millions of dollars. We hear it each year for the major sporting events like the Super Bowl or the Final Four, when major political conventions are held, and when the annual rodeo comes to town. We hear it whenever a major employer shuts down, or is threatening to. We hear it when a city is chosen for the Olympics or the site for the new Toyota plant is announced.

Overall economic impact can be demonstrated in several ways, and probably the most common is to simply take all of the economic activity of the organization (expenditures for the year) and apply the correct economic multiplier to it. Technically, this is a correct economic impact, officially approved by economists. The methodology is presented in the next chapter, but it literally can be as simple as this:

> Current spending of $1.2 million per year is estimated to create $2.34 million worth of commerce (final demand) in the area.

What the preceding method fails to demonstrate is the value of prevention, future outcomes enhanced, costs avoided, and so on, which are the core issues an OVP methodology specifically addresses. A more useful impact is the summary page of an actual OVP. Exhibit 7.7 is the tally of all the separate areas previously accounted for in an OVP, put on an annual basis, so an annual figure can be derived.

## ■ REFERENCES

Stern, Gary J. *The Drucker Foundation Self Assessment Tool* (New York: Jossey-Bass, 1999).

Smith, Adam. *An Inquiry Into the Nature and Causes of the Wealth of Nations*, ed. Edwin Cannan (New York: Modern Library, 1937, first published in 1776).

Wikipedia. *Occam's Razor*. Accessed February 18, 2007, http://en.wikipedia.org/wiki/Occam's_Razor.

# CHAPTER 8

# Suggested Methodologies

> **JOHN MAYNARD KEYNES** *It (economics) is a method rather than a doctrine, an apparatus of the mind, a technique of thinking which helps its possessor to draw correct conclusions.*

T he methodologies used to develop nonprofit ROI scenarios are borrowed from the disciplines of accounting, finance, and economics. In all cases, we must end up with a product that communicates well to the intended audience, which in some cases means that complicated computations must be simplified and resimplified to make the message stick. This often adds the influences of the consumer behavior and communications fields to the mix. No matter how complicated the calculations may seem, the result allows the value of the outcome to be demonstrated.

## PRESENT VALUE BASICS

The first section presents several methods that are common to many different situations. They can be used to present value of future benefits, as in enhanced earning potential for high school graduates, or they can be slightly changed to present value of the costs avoided, as in the value of prevention. For continuity throughout this section, we will use a simplified example of deciding whether a nonprofit should open another free clinic. However the examples are employed, they all involve the time value of money, a discount rate that reflects risk and the cost of funds, and a series of cash flows.

EXHIBIT 8.1    PROJECTED CASH FLOWS

Cash flow year $1 = t_1 = 10{,}000$
Cash flow year $2 = t_2 = 80{,}000$
Cash flow year $3 = t_3 = 90{,}000$
Cash flow year $4 = t_4 = 100{,}000$
Cash flow year $5 = t_5 = 100{,}000 +$ sold for $200{,}000 = 300{,}000$

## Cash Flows

Perhaps the most difficult part of the entire process of determining value is isolating the cash flows themselves. Cash flows are the periodic (usually annual) outlays required to get the project underway and inflows (benefits) expected over the life of the project. The outlays required to get the project underway are usually the easiest component to estimate. Construction costs, lease arrangements, equipments and so forth, personnel costs, are readily available. In this case, the initial investment in the new clinic is estimated to be $100,000. Since this is a cost, it will be represented as a negative flow:

$$\text{Cost at time zero} = \$100{,}000$$
$$\text{Cash flow at } t_0 = -100{,}000$$

After the clinic is built and operating, is will barely break even the first year, and will then operate comfortably in the black for the next four years. At the end of year five, it will be sold to the local hospital for $200,000. These cash flows are represented in Exhibit 8.1.

## Discount Rates

These cash flows then need to be brought back at a discount rate. Discount rates are like interest rates in reverse. Whereas money grows in a savings account at an interest rate, with the future value being larger, future amounts can be brought back to the present day at a discount rate, with the present value being smaller. When everything is put in present value terms, an apples-to-apples comparison can be conducted.

The correct discount rate to use in the case of nonprofits is a matter of debate. In some cases, where the effects of inflation are the only influence

EXHIBIT 8.2    NET PRESENT VALUE FORMULA

$$NPV = \sum_{t=0}^{n} \frac{CF_t}{(1+k)^t}$$

where $CF_t$ is the cash flow at period t, and k is the cost of capital, or the cost of the money for the organization

incorporated into the analysis, a small rate of 2 to 4 percent is appropriate, in 2007 dollars. When the risk of repayment, or default risk, is included, the rate increases appropriately. The actual cost of the money used for the project is also included, but it is important to note that the decision to invest in the project should be separated from the financing decision, or the cost of the money used to pay for the project. Theoretically, the cost of capital for the *firm* should be employed, which is the weighted average of each financing component, and is further discussed in the *Capital Budgeting* section. In this example, we will assume that the cost of capital for the nonprofit is 15.2 percent, and use this number in our analysis.

## Net Present Value

Present value becomes net present value when the initial cost is included, which is usually a negative flow. The basic formula for net present value is presented in Exhibit 8.2.

In English, this translates to the sum of all of the periodic cash flows brought back to today at the appropriate discount rate, as shown in Exhibit 8.3.

EXHIBIT 8.3    NET PRESENT VALUE CALCULATIONS

$$
\begin{aligned}
NPV \text{ (in 000's)} = &- 100 \\
&+ 10/(1 + .152)^1 \\
&+ 80/(1 + .152)^2 \\
&+ 90/(1 + .152)^3 \\
&+ 100/(1 + .152)^4 \\
&+ 300/(1 + .152)^5 \\
\hline
= &\ \$201.80
\end{aligned}
$$

The net present value of this project is $201,800, and since it is a positive number, it should be accepted. The decision rule for net present value methodology is all projected cash flows, brought back to the present at the appropriate discount rate, that reflect the cost of capital for the organization, if the result is positive. As long as the inputs are correct, the $210,800 is a theoretically direct increase in the value of the organization.

## CAPITAL BUDGETING

This entire process can best be illustrated in a capital budgeting example, presented side by side with a for-profit situation. *Capital budgeting* is the term used in the for-profit world to describe how companies analyze projects and decide if investment is merited. It is important to note that the word *capital* in this context describes fixed assets used in production, much as an accountant defines a capital asset. The word *budget* in this context describes inflows and outflows over some defined time period. *Capital budgeting* is a term that describes this entire process, and ends with the decision on which projects should go forward and be included in the capital budget.

Capital budgeting is the process that addresses the investment decision, not the financing decision, and it is important to note the difference. The investment decision is the decision on whether the project should be adopted. It does not describe how funds are raised or the optimal capital structure that minimizes the cost of capital.

The following examples underscore the dramatic differences between NPOs and for-profit organizations in the tools they can employ to help them make better decisions. The first example is a realistic capital budgeting problem that would be faced by a private sector enterprise. The second is a realistic situation for nonprofit, and highlights the problems encountered when private sector methodologies are applied to the nonprofit world.

### Example: Should a Manufacturing Company Buy This New Piece of Equipment?

The XYZ Company is considering the purchase of a piece of equipment that will cost $100. As seen in Exhibit 8.4, it will produce the cash flows for the first five years, and then will be sold for $10 at the end of year five.

EXHIBIT 8.4 **XYZ COMPANY CASH FLOWS**

| Year | 0 | 1 | 2 | 3 | 4 | 5 |
|---|---|---|---|---|---|---|
| Cash flow | −100 | 20 | 30 | 40 | 50 | 50 + 10 sales price |

The cash flows in Exhibit 8.4 are brought back to time zero at the company's weighted average cost of capital, based on Exhibit 8.5. These five years of cash flows brought back at 9.1 percent yield a present value of $ 44.32, so the project should be accepted, since it will add to the overall value of the firm. This example is a simplification of the actual process, since the cash flow inputs and equity cost estimates involve quite a bit of effort. There may also be less quantifiable, but nonetheless important, reasons to accept the project. These include maintaining market share, wanting to be a market innovator, competitive advantage, and so on. The bottom line is that if the inputs are correct, the decision to buy the equipment will add to the value of the firm.

## Example: Should the NPO Open Another Free Clinic?

The XYZ nonprofit is considering opening a third free clinic. The demand is there, but it will cost $100,000 to open. Once opened, it will be

EXHIBIT 8.5 **XYZ COMPANY CAPITAL STRUCTURE**

**Capital structure**
Percentage of equity        60% (common stock)
Percentage of debt        40% (bonds)

**Cost of capital**
Cost of equity        12% (the methods to arrive at this number vary)
Cost of debt        8%

Corporate tax rate        40%

Weighted average cost of capital = weight of debt × cost of debt × (1 − tax rate)
           + weight of equity × cost of equity

Weighted average cost of capital = 40% × 8% × (1 − 40%) + (60% × 12%) = 9.1%

**EXHIBIT 8.6    XYZ NONPROFIT CASH FLOWS**

| Year | 0 | 1 | 2 | 3 | 4 | 5 |
|---|---|---|---|---|---|---|
| Cash flow (in 000's) | −100 | −10 | 80 | 90 | 100 | 100 + 200 sales price |

These cash flows are brought back to time zero at the organization's weighted average cost of capital, based on Exhibit 8.7.

---

self-sustaining. XYZ feels that it can raise the needed $100,000 through a capital campaign, but the cost of that effort will be $20,000. The clinic will be sold at the end of year five to a local hospital for $200,000.

The cash flows of this project are demonstrated in Exhibit 8.6 and are brought back to time zero at the organization's weighted average cost of capital, based on Exhibit 8.7.

The cash flows brought back at 15.2 percent yield a present value of $201,800, so the project should be accepted, since it will add to the overall value of the firm. Now the theoretical questions:

1. Can one equate the cost of equity in a for-profit firm with the cost of raising funds in a nonprofit?

2. Does a target capital structure have any meaning in a nonprofit company?

3. Should a nonprofit accept any project if the net present value is positive, even if the cost of raising the funds is very high?

**EXHIBIT 8.7    XYZ NONPROFIT CAPITAL STRUCTURE**

**Capital structure**

| | |
|---|---|
| Percentage of equity | 60% |
| Percentage of debt | 40% (loans from the local bank) |

**Cost of capital**

| | |
|---|---|
| Cost of equity | 20% (fundraising costs to raise $100,000) |
| Cost of debt | 8% |
| Tax rate | None |

Weighted average cost of capital = weight of debt × cost of debt × (1 − tax rate)
+ weight of equity × cost of equity

Weighted average cost of capital = 40% × 8% × (1 − 0) + (60% × 20%) = 15.2%

These questions can be debated ad nauseum and, unfortunately, some will choose to do so.

# PRESENT VALUE OF FUTURE BENEFITS

Furthering the free clinic example, we have shown that it is a sound financial decision. Let us now bring in the value of the benefits the decision will provide. The clinic can be expected to serve about 3,500 people per year. While all types of medical situations will be addressed, in this particular locale, diabetes is the most common medical condition, and makes up about one-third of all patient visits for the clinic.

Besides the obvious benefit of catching the condition early, thereby preventing much more serious and costly treatment, another benefit of early screening and testing for diabetes is that fewer days of work are missed. In the example in Exhibit 8.8, the benefits to the local economy because of fewer days missed are illustrated.

In other words, approximately $1.36 million could be injected into the local economy because of early detections and proper treatment of

## EXHIBIT 8.8    THE COST OF HYPERTENSION

Start with an actual count of 1,148 patients last calendar year with hypertension.

Step 1    Subtract the number over 65 years old, since they are not likely to be considered part of the full-time workforce:

$$1,148 - 92 = 1,056$$

Step 2    Subtract those not likely to be working by multiplying by the county labor force participation rate of 66.1%:

$$1,056 \times .661 = 698$$

Step 3    Using a county-specific average weekly wage of $440 times 52 weeks per year yields an average annual wage of $22,880.

Step 4    698 patients likely to be working times $22,880 in earnings per year yields $15,973,026 in total earnings for the entire group of patients.

Step 5    Using a national medical journal report that found that those with hypertension who did not benefit from early detection or proper medication had annual earnings 8.5% lower due to complications and missed work compared to those who did receive early detection and medication:

$$\$15,973,026 \times 8.5\% = \$1,357,707 \text{ in lost earnings avoided}$$

| EXHIBIT 8.9 | PRESENT VALUE OF AVOIDED LOST EARNINGS |

$$\$1.36/(1+.152)^{1}$$
$$+\$1.36/(1+.152)^{2}$$
$$+\$1.36/(1+.152)^{3}$$
$$+\$1.36/(1+.152)^{4}$$
$$+\$1.36/(1+.152)^{5}$$

$$= \$4.54 \text{ million}$$

hypertension because of this particular clinic in this particular county. There are several ways to use this information:

**Apply It to a Larger Number of Patients Served**  For every 1,148 patients served, $1.36 million in lost earnings are avoided, or $1,183 per person per year. If the clinic could ramp up to serve 2,000 patients per year, lost earnings avoided would total $2.37 million per year.

**Calculate the Present Value of Several Years**  The $1.36 million in avoided earnings lost can be present valued back to arrive at a value today. If looking for a five-year value, Exhibit 8.9 using a discount rate of 15.2 percent, yields a present value of $4.54 million.

**Demonstrate What it Means to Specific Businesses**  As shown in Exhibit 8.10, the $1.36 million in lost earnings avoided can be further massaged to produce local business impacts.

## Present Valuing Cost Savings

Cost savings manifest themselves in many ways in a health care environment, with the savings provided by preventative measures being common. In the clinic's case, the 3,500 patients per year seen by the clinic include 1,192 adults who have no health insurance. This group is less likely to seek preventative care, and often the disease or ailment is in the more advanced stage by the time they get to the clinic for care. Studies like the one in Exhibit 8.11 have shown that preventative care of the uninsured can reduce total hospital stay days by 3.9 percent and costs by $3,300 per patient.

| EXHIBIT 8.10 | CALCULATING LOCAL CONSUMER EXPENDITURES |

Step 1    Using a gross earnings number of $1.36 million, subtract 30% for the amount of money expected to be spent outside the area:

$$\begin{array}{r} \$1,357,707 \\ -407,312 \\ \hline \$950,395 \end{array}$$

Step 2    Subtract the amount estimated to be taken out for federal and state taxes:

$$\begin{array}{r} \$950,395 \\ -152,063 \\ \hline \$798,332 \end{array}$$

Step 3    Subtract 3% for savings (optimistic) and 3.5% for interest and transfer payments:

$$\begin{array}{r} \$798,332 \\ -28,512 \\ -33,264 \\ \hline \$736,556 \end{array}$$

Step 4    Use the $736,556 as the amount that is actually spent in the local community, possibly in a spending model as presented in Chapter 10, Exhibit 10.5, Local Consumer Expenditures.

| EXHIBIT 8.11 | PRESENT VALUE OF HOSPITAL COSTS |

Step 1          1,192 uninsured adults × 3.9% = 46 hospital stay days reduced

Step 2          46 stay days × $3,300 cost savings per stay day reduced
                = $153,374 total value of preventable stay days

Step 3          5 years of savings of $153,374 present valued back at 15.2%
                = $511,708

# MULTIPLIER EFFECTS

Those who have never been exposed to econometrics are often not familiar with input-output multipliers or how useful they actually can be. Multipliers simply measure the so-called ripple effect, and as shown in Chapter 1, demonstrate the greater effect an economic action has on the economy. An initial economic action causes another economic action to occur, with each action cumulatively adding to the impact of those that come before it. Multipliers are most often presented in the categories of employment, earnings, and output.

The relative unfamiliarity of using multipliers in the nonprofit world may stem from "consultant speak," the deliberate use of jargon and purposely unfamiliar words to protect methods or knowledge, so a higher fee can be charged, or to just look smart. The federal government, which produces a widely used set of multipliers named RIMS II, seems to engage in this practice, too. Notice its description of multipliers from its own Web site:

> Effective planning for public- and private-sector projects and programs at the State and local levels requires a systematic analysis of the economic impacts of these projects and programs on affected regions. In turn, systematic analysis of economic impacts must account for the inter-industry relationships within regions because these relationships largely determine how regional economies are likely to respond to project and program changes. Thus, regional input-output (I-O) multipliers, which account for interindustry relationships within regions, are useful tools for conducting regional economic impact analysis.

It gets even better:

> The RIMS II method for estimating regional I-O multipliers can be viewed as a three-step process. In the first step, the producer portion of the national I-O table is made region-specific by using six-digit NAICS location quotients (LQ's). The LQs estimate the extent to which input requirements are supplied by firms within the region. RIMS II uses LQs based on two types of data: BEA's personal income data (by place of residence) are used to calculate LQs in the service industries; and BEA's wage-and-salary data (by place of work) are used to calculate LQs in the nonservice industries.
>
> In the second step, the household row and the household column from the national I-O table are made region-specific. The household row coefficients, which are derived from the value-added row of the national I-O table, are adjusted to reflect regional earnings leakages resulting from individuals working in the region but residing outside the region. The household column coefficients, which are based on the personal consumption expenditure column of the national I-O table, are adjusted

to account for regional consumption leakages stemming from personal taxes and savings.

The coup de gras:

In the last step, the Leontief inversion approach is used to estimate multipliers. This inversion approach produces output, earnings, and employment multipliers, which can be used to trace the impacts of changes in final demand on directly and indirectly affected industries.

Do not let these paragraphs camouflage the usefulness of multipliers in demonstrating nonprofit ROI. Using them involves only simple math. In the following examples, one can see how easy the use of multipliers can be.

**Example 1 Employment Multipliers**   The nonprofit that runs the medical clinics has a staff of 37 people. The employment multiplier for this county for physicians and health practitioner offices is 1.51:

$$37 \times 1.51 = 56 \text{ jobs}$$

These 37 jobs cause an additional 19 jobs to be created in the local economy because of the ripple effect. Shopping at the grocery store by one of the organization's employees causes a small portion of a grocery store job to be necessary. The grocery store job causes a small portion of a bakery delivery truck driver's job to be necessary. The delivery truck driver causes a small portion of a baker's job to be necessary. The baker's job causes a small portion of a wheat farmer's job to be necessary. You get the picture.

**Example 2 Earnings Multipliers**   This same nonprofit pays $1,640,000 in earnings per year to its employees. The earnings multiplier for this county for physicians and health practitioner offices is 1.27:

$$\$1,640,000 \times 1.27 = \$2,082,800$$

The original $1,640,000 in earnings ripples out into the local economy to the tune of over $2 million in total economic impact.

**Example 3 Output Multipliers**   The total spending of the organization also has an impact. This organization's total budget is $2,650,000 per year. The output multiplier for this county for physicians and health practitioner offices is 1.44:

$$\$2,650,000 \times 1.44 = \$3,816,000$$

The $2.65 million in expenditures per year has an impact of over $3.8 million per year. Note: Output is the one area in which the result is technically termed "output delivered to final demand." This can be somewhat tricky for a service organization, but the results are still a very good approximation of the economic impact of the spending of the organization.

## COMPARISON BASICS

The methods previously presented stand on their own merits, but become even more useful when compared to other measures, such as how much was spent to get the intended result. It is similar to the risk/return tradeoff we have (correctly) heard so often. Hearing that a mutual fund produced a 30 percent return in a given year sounds impressive. It sounds even more impressive when it is compared to the stock market in general, which returned 12 percent that same year. It is most impressive when one introduces the relatively low risk taken to get those impressive results. Without some frame of reference, absolute performance metrics do little to provide a true indication of how an investment, or anything for that matter, actually performed.

## RETURN RATIOS

Return ratios allow a comparison of the value of the outcome to be compared to how much was spent to get it. Two of the most common examples are impact compared to monies expended, and impact compared to the number of people receiving the benefit.

### Impact per Dollar Spent

This inward-looking comparison is most useful when an organization's constituency does not realize the far-reaching effect a program may have. When using economic multipliers, for instance, multipliers are by definition above 1.0, since an economic action will always create some sort of ripple larger than itself. A social service organization, for example, will have an economic impact of at least a dollar of impact for every dollar spent. It is not unusual for these ratios to be 15 to 1, especially when incorporating prevention values or long-term benefits.

## Impact per Person Served

When comparing a large economic impact number to a small universe of direct recipients, the ratios also get quite impressive. This top-down ratio divides the more macro impacts such as the value of medication distributed by the number of recipients, which is useful in demonstrating just how much benefit is delivered on a personal level. The health and education fields are especially fertile areas for this type of comparison.

## ■ REFERENCES

"Regional Multipliers from the Regional Input-Output Modeling System (RIMS II): A Brief Description." Last updated March 6, 2007. Accessed March 16, 2007, http://www.bea.gov/regional/rims/brfdesc.cfm.

# Communicating an ROI-Based Program

## TREATING INVESTORS AS INVESTORS

One cannot fully adopt the investment-driven concept without actually treating investors as investors. This means really treating them as people who gave you their hard-earned dollars in return for fulfilling their values or providing value to them. They deserve to be kept informed on how their investment is performing.

Less than stellar results, or simply not performing at projected levels, often cause NPOs to shy away from reporting their results. This can be a fatal flaw in the investment-driven framework. Investors understand that things do not always go as planned, especially in an initiative that spans four or five years.

One trap to avoid at all costs is using the excuse of not having enough funding as the reason why projected results were not achieved. Few, if any, NPOs have all the money they feel they need. This is a universal given in the

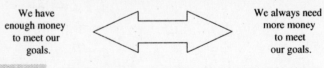

We have
enough money
to meet our
goals.

We always need
more money
to meet
our goals.

EXHIBIT 9.1    **The Two Camps of Funding and Meeting
One's Goals**

nonprofit arena, but it cannot be used as an excuse without alienating investors. Experience has shown that NPOs can be split into two camps on this issue, with some falling in between the extremes, as shown in Exhibit 9.1.

Let's not confuse the issue. Those who have enough money to meet their goals are not saying they have all the money they need, simply that they were good budgeters and planners and did not let their reach exceed their grasp. They have the confidence they will deliver, and are much more likely to not be afraid to publish their progress, even if it was not as much as they would like.

Those in the group of always using the lack of funding as an excuse for not accomplishing their goals are usually not good planners, budgeters, or sometimes even managers. This point is not lost on outside funders. Because they do not reach the goals set out for them given a certain level of resources, they are not likely to want to publish their progress, whether in a newsletter, annual report, or in anything for that matter.

## THE IMPORTANCE OF AN INVESTOR
## RELATIONS PROGRAM

The function of *investor relations* is not something to be taken lightly, especially after one has raised a large amount of money through a capital or annual campaign, or received that unexpected multimillion-dollar bequest no one knew was coming. We normally see this function tacked onto the job description of the communications person, which can work well, but it does need to be a priority. Simply adding it as a line item on a job description does not ensure that it gets properly done. In the case of those NPOs that have completely adopted the investment-driven model, they have actually changed the communications person's position title to Director of Investor Relations, or simply Investor Relations.

An Investor Relations program in the for-profit world serves the purpose of keeping investors in the loop of what is happening within the company, to ensure that no surprises, especially bad ones, that will dramatically lower stock price suddenly make the six o'clock news. Their job is to keep their investors happy and informed, since stockholders, who actually own the company, are their bosses.

It is not any different in the nonprofit world, or let's say, it *should* not be any different. Are the investors the boss? Literally, no; figuratively, yes. Are investors the owners of the organization? Legally, no; figuratively, yes. Do investors want to be surprised at the end of the year that goals were not met? No and no. To be sure, there is no stock price that will plummet because profit levels were not met and everyone rushed to unload the stock. However, are there investors who will not reinvest because certain goals were not accomplished?

## Communicating Your Results

How ROI is communicated can be just as important as what is communicated—supporting the *medium is the message* mantra. There is no one right way to do it, just as there is no one right way to advertise. What need to be present, though, are credibility, objectivity, and regularity.

**Credibility**   Once credibility is lost, it really will not matter how good the results are, since nobody will believe them anyway. One of the most common reasons credibility is lost is by results that are too good to be true and, therefore, simply not believable. Taking credit where credit is not due undermines the entire process.

The most common attacks on credibility come in the various forms of the following statements and questions:

- That would have happened anyway.
- You can't take credit for that.
- Three of four groups in the local area are taking credit for the same thing.
- How much of that (the result in question) can you take credit for?

Dealing with these potential credibility assaults must be preemptive, and is a two-step process.

1. Make sure the issue passes the "reasonableness test." That is, would an average person armed with the facts agree with your particular organization getting credit (maybe not all of the credit, but a significant portion of the credit)?

2. Make sure the results reported are not so off the charts that they become unbelievable. While the return per dollar invested can be very large when dealing with prevention, education, and downstream impact, it is important to use a straightforward methodology that can be easily explained.

**Objectivity**    Closely related to credibility, results that are not independently verifiable are immediately suspected. For example, if one is using local data, such as wage levels, in the computation of ROI, the wage levels should be verifiable. Publicly available information should be used when possible to allow independent verification should someone choose to do so. Sources should be stated and not so obscure that they cannot be easily found.

"Every nonprofit does a great job; just ask them." This statement has been used in our seminars for years. It is followed up with, "How many of you do a bad job?" Rarely do hands ever shoot up into the air. It is for these same reasons why independent, outside professionals are often used to produce ROI reports. It is similar to the small business that has a bookkeeper in house to do payroll, pay bills, and so on, but when it comes time to do the taxes, they hire an outside CPA firm to sign their tax return. The objectivity provided by an outside firm can be invaluable, and the level of expertise should be much higher.

**Regularity**    This is akin to frequency in the advertising world. The message is of little value if it is not reinforced and heard often. Quarterly Investor Reports should be the standard, especially if the organization has just raised millions of dollars under an investment-driven format.

Continuous reporting is important. The urge to report results just prior to launching another round of funding is better than not reporting at all, but it is then seen by investors as a thinly veiled prelude to being asked for more money and not as true reporting.

# EXAMPLES

There are many ways to report ROI, with some being more creative than others. Sometimes the goal is broader awareness of the organization; sometimes it is in the course of a fundraising campaign. Three widely varying examples of how nonprofits have done this are presented.

## Special Event Program

The Impact Group (formerly the Gwinnett Housing Resource Partnership) in Duluth, Georgia, throws an annual Monopoly® Gala Event where guests "buy, beg, borrow, trade, or steal" fictitious property, as if the entire room were playing one huge game of Monopoly®. This event is appropriate for this nonprofit since they are in the business of reducing homelessness, educating future homeowners, and revitalizing entire neighborhoods. Exhibit 9.2 illustrates how just a small portion of the program for the event was used to remind people of their impact on the community.

## Newsletter

The folks at the Northwest Georgia Healthcare Partnership, after working with our company on a sustainability plan, took the ROI portion very seriously. As shown in their 2006 newsletter in Exhibit 9.3, they do a fine job of quantifying eight separate areas of impact. When compared to their annual budget, they are claiming a 48-to-1 return, or 4,800 percent. In 2005, this newsletter claiming a return of 15-to-1 was accompanied by an annual appeal for funding. Results like these that are so positive often lead investors to question the methodology, but it certainly sets up a reason to talk to investors and discuss it.

## Investors Report

The most ROI-focused version of an investor relations effort is an ROI Report. As shown in Exhibit 9.4 for Grand Junction, Colorado, they are not shy about putting their performance out there for all investors to see. In fact, this type of report is done regularly for their investors, and builds the credibility needed when a new funding campaign needs to be launched.

Established in 1992, Gwinnett Housing Resource Partnership has made an IMPACT! on Gwinnett each year.

- GHRP impacts businesses . . . $21.8 million every year
- GHRP impacts the larger local economy . . . $26.6 million per year
- GHRP creates a stronger community . . . $15.6 million per year
- GHRP d/b/a **The IMPACT! Group** impacts you!
    - o    $64 million total per year
    - o    $19 return for every $1 we spend

**The IMPACT! Group** . . .
                one of the best investments you can make!

**Washington Mutual**

Presents

Gwinnett Housing
Resource Partnership's
2nd Annual

**MONOPOLY**
Gwinnett MONOPOLY Gala

October 16, 2004
Gwinnett Center
7:00 p.m.

**EXHIBIT 9.2    Impact Group Special Event Brochure**

# BUT WHAT HAPPENS IN FOUR YEARS?

A common question heard in sustainability planning is, "What happens in four years?" This refers to the fact that plans are typically presented as four-year plans with four-year price tags. When the four years are over, and results are delivered, then what happens? If the investment-driven model was used, the answer is easy: Investors should be asked to reinvest. And they will if the previous investment was a good one.

As a personal matter, if one invests in real estate and makes some money on it, one is likely to do it again. If one invests in technology stocks and makes a killing in the stock market, one is likely to try it again. If one buys classic cars

NORTHWEST
GEORGIA
HEALTHCARE
PARTNERSHIP

Executive Summary of
Outcome Projections for Projects
Incubated by the Healthcare Partnership

## What is the benefit of promoting good health?

**CRITICAL Conditions**
- Advanced directives = prevented costs                             $ 1,607,710

**Boys & Girls Club**
- High graduation rate = higher earnings                            1,144,720
- Low drop-out rate = lower public assistance                       89,100

**Promotores de Salud**
- Prenatal care = full-term births                                  562,400
- Diabetes care management = fewer hospitalizations                  75,708
- Diabetes care management = reduced risk of amputation             67,467

**MedBank**
- Dollar value of medications provided                              3,792,584
- Cost savings due to medication compliance                         15,246,188

                                                                    $22,585,877


**Healthcare Partnership's 2006 budget:              $     463,662**
**Annualized cost prevented / services provided:  $ 22,585,877**

### Annual Return on Investment: 48:1

It should be noted that these are only eight examples of work developed by the Healthcare
Partnership. Other activities equally important but not readily measurable include many, many
hours of promoting exercise, diet and healthy lifestyles.

*OUR MISSION:*
*To develop and support cooperation and collaboration*
*between health care providers, business, industry, payers,*
*social organizations, government, educators and the community*
*for the purpose of improving the health of all*
*through the efficient, effective, and caring use of resources*

**EXHIBIT 9.3    Northwest Georgia Healthcare Partnership
Newsletter**

# Return On Investment Report

**Grand Junction Economic Partnership**          *August 2005*

## PROGRAM IMPACTS

### Investment Reality

| | |
|---|---|
| Total Program Expenditures 1990 - 2005 | $ 4,531,302 |
| Weighted Average Earnings per Job | $ 28,992 |
| Average Development Group earnings multiplier | 1.7192 |
| Earnings Impact of Average Job | $ 48,369 |
| *Breakeven number of jobs* | 94 |
| *(Job Impact to Expenditures 2001 to 2004)* | |

### Return Ratios

Based on 2001-2004 Total Program Expenditures:

| | |
|---|---|
| Direct Earnings Returned | 15 to 1 |
| *Total Impact* Earnings Returned | 26 to 1 |

### Ripple Effect

**Employment**   Every job created creates. 94 new jobs

**Earnings**   Every dollar paid in earnings creates
$ 72 in new earnings

## Salary Comparison

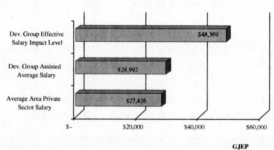

| | |
|---|---|
| Dev. Group Effective Salary Impact Level | $48,369 |
| Dev. Group Assisted Average Salary | $28,992 |
| Average Area Private Sector Salary | $27,426 |

$-        $20,000        $40,000        $60,000

### Grand Junction Area

Total Employment
| | |
|---|---|
| January 1990 | 40,578 |
| August 2005 | 66,035 |
| Jobs created | 25,457 |

| Development Group assisted companies | |
|---|---|
| Direct Employment | 2,420 |
| Total Impact Employment | 4,203 |

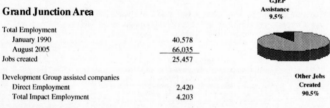

GJEP
Assistance
9.5%

Other Jobs
Created
90.5%

**EXHIBIT 9.4**    **Grand Junction Economic Partnership Report**

on the cheap, rebuilds them, and resells them at a much higher price, that person is likely to keep rebuilding cars. If investors in nonprofits see the results they desire, whether in things they value *or* in value itself, they will also reinvest.

When working with nonprofits, we normally suggest repackaging sustainability plans, business plans, and strategic plans (or whatever title one chooses) as *strategic investment initiatives* to denote the following nuances:

1. *Strategic* connotes long-term planning.

2. *Investment* introduces the concept that results are expected.

3. *Initiative* implies the future plan is not business as usual.

The importance of this is that if it was introduced as an investment, and the results are delivered, more investment for more results should be automatic.

## UNCONVENTIONAL WISDOM

Both conventional and unconventional wisdom have their place, but if the reader has gotten this far in the book, it should come as no surprise that unconventional wisdom has a more prominent spot in this text.

1. If you want to catch some fish, you have to use the right bait.

    What is the right bait these days? It's ROI. It's the answer to "What's in it for me?" If this sounds too cold for the warm-and-fuzzy world of nonprofits, then you have either:

    (a) Cultivated your investors to the point that they trust the organization to deliver on its mission. Congratulations!

    (b) Left money on the table, because there are people, organizations, and foundations that will invest in results.

    ROI simply gets you to the top of the list.

2. Culture beats strategy, every time!

    This cliché is very true in the fundraising process. An example is appropriate:

    In these days of high gas prices, concerns for energy, global warming, care of the earth, and so on, SUVs have fallen out of favor. Detroit does not like this, but it is reality.

    The culture is that cost of ownership and fuel efficiency now matter. The moral of the story: The strategy to build the biggest, baddest, boldest SUV does not matter anymore. The culture has made that strategy obsolete, or at least not profitable. Culture beats strategy, every time.

Another example:

You walk into a foundation that has a habit of making 10 grants of $50,000 or less per year. Their internal culture is to make many small investments. Your request of $250,000 is going to do two things:

(a) Verify the fact that you did not do your research on the foundation's giving patterns.

(b) Put your request at risk of being thrown out completely.
    Your strategy to get $250,000, no matter how well thought out, will not beat the culture of the foundation.

3.  Even if you are on the right track, you will get run over if you just sit there.

This is one of Will Rogers's best quotes, and is so relevant. Many organizations view the writing of a Sustainability Plan or an annual ROI reporting as the job being completed. It is a source of constant amazement how much blood, sweat, and tears executives put into these documents, only to then view the process as finished! Writing the document is the easy part. Putting it into action is the hard part, but the part that gets investors motivated to fund the organization.

## ▣ REFERENCES

Impact Group Gala Program, 2004.
Northwest Georgia Healthcare Partnership Newsletter Executive Summary, 2006.
Grand Junction Economic Partnership ROI Report, August 2005.

# CHAPTER 10

# Putting OVP to Work:
# ROI Profiles

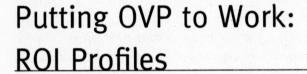

**AUTHOR UNKNOWN** *If wishes were horses, beggars would ride.*

T he following eight examples were pulled from our client files to represent the wide variety of ways in which ROI can be used. Sometimes they rely heavily on demonstrating value for funding purposes, sometimes it is used as a framework for decision-making, and sometimes it is used to enhance credibility. All relevant detail is included, and the situations are presented as realistically as possible without revealing the client's name or identifying information.

## ORGANIZATION 1: RURAL, SMALL, AND DEPENDENT ON GRANTS

### Profile

| | |
|---|---|
| Type of organization | 501 (c) (3) |
| Annual budget | $1 million to $3 million |
| Staff size | 26 to 50 |
| Area of emphasis | Community health |
| Years in operation | 1 to 10 |
| Geographic area | Southeastern United States |

## Background

This organization started with a small planning grant and three years of operational funding. After this initial period was over, they needed new sources of funding. As with most NPOs, there was constant effort expended on writing grants, but at one point, the future-minded director decided that a capital campaign was in order.

Being very limited in money available for outside fundraising counsel, much of the work was done by staff, augmented with additional professional coaching. Our firm was called on to help develop the ROI case for support. While at first there was the assumption that we would have to dig for data and be creative with the OVP, we were pleasantly surprised to find extremely good records and large amounts of data with which to work.

This NPO works primarily with teenage pregnancy and adolescent mothers on several levels. First, they did their part to educate the community on the dangers and consequences of teenage pregnancy. If an area teen became pregnant, they worked to make sure she received the proper prenatal care so the baby was born healthy. Once the baby was born, they provided quality care so the mother could continue her education. They helped the mother with counseling and training to deal with the difficult realities of the situation. Last, they made sure the new mother succeeded in graduating high school or receiving a GED certificate.

## Primary Use of ROI/OVP Material

- Build credibility.
- Document prior results.
- Entice investment.

## The ROI Framework

The framework for the ROI case was presented in the following categories:

- Opportunity costs of not graduating
- Value of childcare services provided
- Transportation services provided
- Low birthweight baby prevention savings
- Second unwanted births prevention savings

- Value of counseling services provided
- Crisis intervention services provided
- Entity impacts

## Value Proposition Presented

Information was presented in each of the preceding categories in both their campaign brochure and their annual report that year. Since the campaign was structured as a four-year initiative, the impacts were presented within a four-year time frame. Exhibit 10.1 illustrates how the value was presented in the campaign brochure.

## Takeaway Message

The message of their ROI case was crafted around the fact that if the organization had to close its doors due to lack of funding, a $10 million hole

**EXHIBIT 10.1    OVP INFORMATION PRESENTED IN CAMPAIGN BROCHURE**

| | 4-Year Impact |
|---|---|
| **Educational impacts** | |
| Earnings opportunity costs of not graduating | $1,050,000 |
| 5 students per year graduating high school or obtaining a GED | |
| Value of child care services | $1,352,160 |
| 36 available openings per year | |
| Transportation for GED students, actual costs | $86,080 |
| **Health care impacts** | |
| Low birthweight prevention savings | $932,136 |
| 1 low birthweight and 2 very low birthweight babies prevented per year | |
| Societal costs of teen pregnancy saved—3 second births prevented per year | $510,000 |
| Counseling provided to families and individuals, market value of 2,100 hours provided per year | $546,000 |
| Crisis intervention services, actual costs | $91,440 |
| **Organizational impacts** | |
| Annual earnings impact of $1,322,772 | $5,291,088 |
| **Total 4-year initiative value to the community** | **$9,858,904** |

would be left in the community. This $10 million value could be secured by a community investment of $2 million, resulting in a five-to-one return.

## ORGANIZATION 2: GOOD TRACK RECORD, BUT NOT WELL KNOWN

### Profile

| | |
|---|---|
| Type of organization | 501 (c) (3) |
| Annual budget | $500,000 to $1 million |
| Staff size | 1 to 10 |
| Area of emphasis | Rural health |
| Years in operation | 11 to 25 |
| Geographic area | Eastern United States |

### Background

This organization began operating in the mid-1990s with the goal of improving access to health care in the underserved areas of the state. Over time, this has included such varied efforts as:

- Leadership development in rural communities
- Rural health network development
- Access to capital
- Technical assistance
- Recruitment and retention of health providers

Early funding came primarily from foundation grants, with subsequent funding from both state and federal sources. Much of what the organization is known for, and what sets it apart, is its loan program that allows projects in rural areas to be financed that otherwise would not be realized. Projects range from the construction of new facilities such as doctors' offices, to specialized equipment, to refinancing. The organization is extremely adept at levering resources and involving financing partners that allow the financing risk to be shared.

## Primary Use of ROI/OVP Material

- Document prior results.
- Demonstrate value.
- Position for increased private sector investment.

## The ROI Framework

The framework for demonstrating value was presented in the following categories:

### Financing Impacts

- Overall impacts derived from the financing activity itself
- Business-to-business impacts from lending activity

### Client Operations Impacts

- Downstream impacts from the client operations
- Local business impacts from client operations

Client impacts were determined on a case-by-case basis, and used client expenditures, employment, and payroll information to determine respective impacts.

## Value Proposition Presented

The preceding information was distilled into two major categories:

| | |
|---|---|
| 1. Aggregate client operations impact | $89,478,954 |
|     Representative share of annual client organization impact | |
| 2. Loan fund financing-impact | $4,423,935 |
|     $19.9 million/4.5-year time period | |
| Total Annual Impact | $93,902,889 |

## Takeaway Message

Demonstrating the downstream impacts that would not have occurred if the NPO did not step in to make the initial project happen, through access to capital, leveraging, and the technical assistance necessary to pull all of the pieces together, positioned the organization as a pivotal player in improving access to health care throughout the rural areas of the state. Its conservatively estimated impact of almost $94 million provided a return on invested dollars of almost 13 to 1.

## ORGANIZATION 3: DEMONSTRATING IMPORTANCE TO THE COMMUNITY

### Profile

| | |
|---|---|
| Type of organization | 501 (c) (3) |
| Annual budget | $1 million to $3 million |
| Staff size | 11 to 25 |
| Area of emphasis | Housing |
| Years in operation | 11 to 25 |
| Geographic area | Eastern United States |

### Background

This organization is in the business of constructing affordable housing in existing low- to moderate-income residential areas. They had built over 200 houses in the past, and were now looking to become more aggressive in their approach. Their new focus was to actually build neighborhoods, rather than one or two houses at a time.

Their initiative included expenses for:

- Architectural design
- Landscaping design
- Real estate
- Construction of up to 100 new homes

### Primary Use of ROI/OVP Material

- Demonstrate impact.
- Illustrate wide spectrum of ROI.
- Entice investment.

### The ROI Framework

While there are many sources for information on the various values of homeownership, the NPO wanted to move beyond the anecdotal and present what it might mean in dollars and cents. The framework for demonstrating value was presented in the following categories:

- Construction impact
- Development/infrastructure impact
- Property tax impact
- Utilities impact (electricity, gas, water, telephone, cable television)
- Property insurance impact
- Expenditures by homeowners

## Value Proposition Presented

Four of the categories, and the accompanying explanations, are presented here:

1. Home Construction Impact: $12.1 million
   This amount includes the economic activity in all of the industries that are part of the construction process, including materials, subcontractors, labor, etc. Applying a multiplier of 2.4, construction spending of $4,975,000 grows to over $12,066,000 in impact.

2. Land Development: $5.5 million
   This amount reflects the economic activity due to road construction, water and sewer lines, etc. The estimated investment of $2,268,500 impacts the area similar to construction expenditures, and grows to an impact of $5,501,000 when ripple effects are considered.

3. Real Estate: $439,834
   This amount includes the average 6.5-percent commissions earned in the local real estate industry if the homes are sold in the local market at construction costs alone of $50,000. This amount increases to $1.15 million if the homes are sold at an estimated market of $130,000 each.

4. Local Taxes: $156,130 per year
   Local taxes can be expected to increase $156,130 per year, based on the prevailing effective tax rate of $12.01 per $1,000 of valuation, with valuation-based home market values of $130,000 each.

## Takeaway Message

The message moved those considering investing in the organization from a mindset of a house here and a house there to one of entire neighborhoods being revitalized. Special consideration was given to the public sector, which would realize increased tax revenues for years to come.

## ORGANIZATION 4: LARGE AND WELL KNOWN, BUT CAMPAIGN HAS STALLED

### Profile

| | |
|---|---|
| Type of organization | 501 (c) (3) |
| Annual budget | $3 million to $10 million |
| Staff size | 11 to 25 |
| Area of emphasis | Children |
| Years in operation | 11 to 25 |
| Geographic area | Southeastern United States |

### Background

This organization was in the middle of a $17 million capital campaign when they decided that an OVP would give the campaign the boost they needed to reach their funding goal. Their work with area youth covered four separate facilities, for which the campaign would provide needed repairs and updating. The expansion of the facilities would provide the capacity to serve over 5,000 new members.

The organization had great data to work with and some wonderful stories to tell. They used a variety of fundraising efforts, including annual campaigns, special events, and planned giving. Projects and emphasis were on providing a safe and structured environment for children, with sports and organized activities comprising many of the organization's efforts.

### Primary Use of ROI/OVP Material

- Illustrate wide spectrum of ROI.
- Demonstrate value.
- Justify large investments.

### The ROI Framework

The framework for demonstrating value focused on the societal costs avoided and the positive outcomes enhanced was presented in the following categories:

- Reduction in crime costs
- Teen pregnancy costs avoided
- Education impacts

Additionally, the classical economic impact of construction activity and entity impacts were also presented.

## Value Proposition Presented

Comparing the children served by the organization with the greater population in general yielded some impressive results. In the area of crime, for example, the following picture emerged:

Less than 1 percent of members were arrested, which compares to a 14-percent arrest rate in the three-county area served by the NPO. Applying area percentages to members aged 10 to 19, one can reasonably extrapolate that 1,149 members could be expected to be arrested, a number far greater than the actual 9 who were arrested.

The costs of crime can be broken down into two distinct areas: *juvenile justice system costs* and *victim costs avoided*. Applying state estimates to the preceding difference, the value of crime costs avoided is substantial, as shown in Exhibit 10.2.

### EXHIBIT 10.2    VALUE OF LOWER CRIME

| | |
|---|---|
| Juvenile justice system costs per arrest | $9,652 |
| Victim costs avoided per arrest | $4,937 |
| Total cost per arrest | $14,589 |
| Arrests avoided | 1,140 |
| Total value of lower crime costs | $16,625,041 |

Exhibit 10.3 shows the summary impacts that were also presented.

## Takeaway Message

Crafting the value message in broad societal terms allowed the organization to broaden its base of potential investors and provide evidence to critics that their investment actually made a difference. The sheer size of some of the direct impacts in their own community could not be ignored.

EXHIBIT 10.3    **SUMMARY IMPACTS**

|  | Impact |
|---|---|
| **Organizational impacts** | |
| Earnings impacts (annual) | $6,601,735 |
| Employment impact (number of jobs expected annually) | 54 |
| Total output impact | $13,753,713 |
| **Construction impacts** | |
| Total output impact | $16,966,850 |
| Employment impact (number of jobs during construction only) | 195 |
| Earnings impacts (one-time event) | $5,039,650 |
| **Crime impact** | |
| Arrest costs avoided | $16,625,041 |
| **Teen pregnancy impact** | |
| Societal costs avoided (per occurrence, over 20 years) | $331,236 |
| Prevention of annual earnings lost | $ 1,134,000 |
| **Education Impact** | |
| Economic gain of 5,200 new members due to high school graduation | $ 5,857,524 |

# ORGANIZATION 5: LARGE AND WELL KNOWN, BUT ROI NOT OBVIOUS

## Profile

| | |
|---|---|
| Type of organization | 501 (c) (3) |
| Annual budget | $1 million to $3 million |
| Staff size | 11 to 25 |
| Area of emphasis | Health |
| Years in operation | 1 to 10 |
| Geographic area | Southeastern United States |

## Background

This organization had its beginnings as a true public–private partnership. City, county, and the large hospitals in the area banded together to form an organization that could provide health insurance to the uninsured working poor. With heath care costs skyrocketing, and the cost of health insurance rising with it, health insurance was not realistic for many caught in the middle of incomes too high for government programs, but too low to afford private health insurance.

This effort made sense from the perspective of better health for individuals, and from economic development and cost containment perspectives. From the economic development perspective, having an affordable health plan in place would benefit and enhance the labor pool, and from a hospital perspective, it hoped to alleviate some of the pressure on emergency rooms as a provider of last resort for medical care.

The cost to society of the uninsured in general terms is well documented. These were the reasons the program was initiated in the first place. What this NPO desired was something that compared their specific situation and inputs to their specific outcomes.

## Primary Use of ROI/OVP Material

- Document prior results.
- Demonstrate value.

## The ROI Framework

The impact of the NPO's members, or those enrolled in the insurance program, was not known. Questions that were asked included:

- How much do they contribute economically to the area?
- What is the value of these members not missing work due to proper medical care?
- How does preventative care reduce the burden on the area's emergency rooms?

The answers to the first two questions are presented in this profile. Member profiles were analyzed to determine the impact by their income and the industry in which they worked.

The value of one day per month of work not missed was used as a reasonable criterion of the value of access to medical care.

## Value Proposition Presented

The 1,240 insured members earned an average of $20,339 per year. By applying employment and earnings multipliers specific to their respective industry, it was determined that collectively, they injected over $42.1 million in earnings into the economy per year, and their jobs created another 494 jobs in the area.

This $42.1 million in total earnings produced an estimated $24,931,000 in discretionary income in the area. By virtue of participating in the program, savings could be realized in such ways as:

- Not waiting until a condition deteriorated to seek medical attention
- Early detection of preventable illnesses
- Much less likely to be hospitalized (50 to 70 percent) because of early treatment

If just one day per month of missed work was saved on average by members, a figure thought to be conservative, over $1.15 million a year in additional earnings could be injected into the local economy.

## Takeaway Message

Even though members in the program were low-wage earners, their economic impact on the community was substantial. The $1.15 million in earnings not lost by members was approximately equal to the annual cost of the program. When other factors, such as lower emergency room utilization, were factored in, the return to the community was much more than previously realized.

## ORGANIZATION 6: DRILLING DEEP INTO THE PRIVATE SECTOR

### Profile

| | |
|---|---|
| Type of organization | 501 ( c ) (3) |
| Annual budget | $500,000 to $1 million |
| Staff size | 1 to 10 |
| Area of emphasis | Economic development |
| Years in operation | 11 to 25 |
| Geographic area | Eastern United States |

## Background

This economic development organization, as part of their campaign tool chest, wanted to demonstrate the potential local impacts of their future efforts. In other words, they wanted to demonstrate what the local impact would be if they met their objectives. This is a powerful fundraising tool that opens up a completely new set of motivations and fits perfectly with the investment-driven model. They also wanted objective evidence that their efforts and resources that were directed toward recruitment in certain industries had a larger potential impact than focusing on tourism and retail, which are sometimes politically risky decisions.

## Primary Use of ROI/OVP Material

- Build credibility for program.
- Document prior results.
- Use as a solicitation tool.

## The ROI Framework

The framework for demonstrating value contained two separate parts. The first was a bottom-up process, building the total impact from job and earnings inputs. These results were then reduced to a top-down process where the impacts were taken to a local business level. The second compared the impacts of their targeted industries with commensurate retail and tourism impacts.

## Value Proposition Presented

For the first part, using inputs of jobs and earnings within targeted industries, together with area-specific multipliers, net personal consumption expenditures were developed, as shown in Exhibit 10.4.

Net personal consumption expenditures were then used as inputs for a Consumer Spending model; Exhibit 10.5 demonstrates how the earnings from these jobs would ripple throughout the community in local businesses.

For the second part, the four targeted industries were compared to area retail and tourism impact.

EXHIBIT 10.4    DETERMINATION OF CONSUMER EXPENDITURES

| | |
|---|---|
| **Number of new primary jobs** | 3,500 |
| Primary wage rate paid (hourly) | $15.63 |
| Total direct payroll | $109,410,000 |
| **Total payroll** | $132,386,100 |
| **Total jobs** | 4,792 |
| Calculated indirect jobs created | 1,292 |
| Calculated indirect wage rate paid (hourly) | $8.55 |
| **Area values** | |
| Personal income | $92,670,270 |
| Disposable personal income | $78,315,645 |
| **Net personal consumption expenditures** | $73,178,139 |

EXHIBIT 10.5    LOCAL CONSUMER EXPENDITURES

**How the money will likely be spent based on earnings level of target jobs**

| | |
|---|---|
| Projected consumer expenditures | $73,178,139 |
| Expected income range of primary jobs | $20,000 to $29,999 |
| Weighted average annual wage | $31,260 |
| **Area expenditures** | |
| **Food** | $10,933,621 |
| Food at home | $7,198,346 |
| Cereals and bakery products | $1,015,733 |
| Cereals and cereal products | $355,381 |
| Bakery products | $660,352 |
| Meats, poultry, fish, eggs | $2,016,343 |
| Beef | $602,383 |
| Pork | $471,320 |
| Other meats | $239,441 |
| Poultry | $347,819 |
| Fish and seafood | $254,563 |
| Eggs | $103,338 |
| Dairy products | $761,170 |
| Fresh milk and cream | $312,533 |
| Other dairy products | $448,636 |
| Fruits and vegetables | $1,255,174 |
| Fresh fruits | $393,187 |
| Fresh vegetables | $415,871 |
| Processed fruits | $259,604 |
| Processed vegetables | $189,032 |
| Other food at home | $2,147,406 |
| Sugar and other sweets | $277,247 |

**EXHIBIT 10.5**   (Continued)

| | |
|---|---|
| Fats and oils | $201,634 |
| Miscellaneous foods | $995,569 |
| Nonalcoholic beverages | $625,066 |
| Food prepared by consumer unit on out-of-town trips | $50,409 |
| Food away from home | $3,737,796 |
| **Alcoholic beverages** | $622,546 |
| **Housing** | $24,770,777 |
| Shelter | $14,202,618 |
| **Owned dwellings** | $6,810,199 |
| Mortgage interest and charges | $3,241,272 |
| Property taxes | $1,870,158 |
| Maintenance, repairs, insurance, other expenses | $1,696,249 |
| Rented dwellings | $7,006,793 |
| Other lodging | $388,146 |
| Utilities, fuels, and public service | $6,033,907 |
| Natural gas | $819,139 |
| Electricity | $2,270,907 |
| Fuel oil and other fuels | $229,359 |
| Telephone services | $2,046,588 |
| Water and other public services | $667,914 |
| Household operations | $1,043,458 |
| Personal services | $380,585 |
| Other household expenses | $665,393 |
| Housekeeping supplies | $1,073,703 |
| Laundry and cleaning supplies | $307,492 |
| Other household products | $483,922 |
| Postage and stationery | $284,808 |
| Household furnishings and equipment | $2,414,571 |
| Household textiles | $221,798 |
| Furniture | $577,178 |
| Floor coverings | $42,847 |
| Major appliances | $461,239 |
| Small appliances, miscellaneous house wares | $171,389 |
| Miscellaneous household equipment | $937,600 |
| **Apparel and services** | $2,802,717 |
| Men and boys | $514,168 |
| Men, 16 and over | $365,462 |
| Boys, 2 to 15 | $148,705 |
| Women | $1,121,591 |
| Women, 16 and over | $922,477 |
| Girls, 2 to 15 | $199,114 |
| Children under 2 | $166,348 |
| Footwear | $617,505 |
| Other apparel products and services | $383,105 |

*(Continued)*

**EXHIBIT 10.5**   (Continued)

| | |
|---|---|
| **Transportation** | $14,152,209 |
| Vehicle purchases | $6,570,759 |
|   Cars and trucks, new | $3,183,302 |
|   Cars and trucks, used | $3,458,029 |
|   Other vehicles | |
| Gasoline and motor oil | $2,654,012 |
| Other vehicle expenses | $4,249,443 |
|   Vehicles finance charges | $579,699 |
|   Maintenance and repairs | $1,207,286 |
|   Vehicle insurance | $1,837,393 |
|   Vehicles rental, leases, licenses, other charges | $622,546 |
|   Public transportation | $677,995 |
| **Health care** | $5,761,701 |
| Health insurance | $2,999,311 |
| Medical services | $1,136,714 |
| Drugs | $1,348,430 |
| Medical supplies | $279,768 |
| **Entertainment** | $3,823,491 |
| Fees and admissions | $574,658 |
| Television, radios, sound equipment | $1,449,247 |
| Pets, toys, and playground equipment | $1,111,509 |
| Other entertainment supplies, equipment, and services | $688,077 |
| **Personal care products and services** | $967,845 |
| **Reading** | $239,441 |
| **Education** | $632,628 |
| **Tobacco products** | $816,619 |
| **Miscellaneous** | $1,285,419 |
| **Cash contributions** | $2,278,468 |
| **Personal insurance and pensions** | $4,088,136 |
| Life and personal insurance | $546,933 |
| Pensions and Social Security | $3,541,203 |
| **Total** | **$73,175,618** |

Using the 535 jobs, with commensurate wages and multipliers, represented by the four industries included in the analysis, the impact compared to the retail and tourism industries is displayed in Exhibit 10.6.

In other words, as an apples-to-apples comparison of the impact of the same number of jobs, but in different industries with different wage rates and multipliers, the four industries represent the increases shown in Exhibit 10.7 over the retail and tourism sectors.

**EXHIBIT 10.6    INDUSTRY IMPACT COMPARISONS**

| Industry | Jobs | Earnings Impact | Employment Impact |
|---|---|---|---|
| Targeted-industry average | 535 | $31.7 million | 986 |
| Retail | 535 | $12.4 million | 650 |
| Tourism | 535 | $11.8 million | 613 |

**EXHIBIT 10.7    SUMMARY OF TARGET IMPACTS ON OTHER INDUSTRIES**

| | Earnings | Employment |
|---|---|---|
| Increase over retail | +156% | +52% |
| Increase over tourism | +169% | +61% |

## Takeaway Message

The message was clear that the goals of the organization impacted every business and everyone in the area, making them all potential targets for investment in the capital campaign. The message also verified that even though it may be unpopular, the pursuit of targeted industries had a larger and more powerful impact than growing the retail or tourism sectors.

# ORGANIZATION 7: ROI GONE WRONG

## Profile

| | |
|---|---|
| Type of organization | 501 (c) (3) |
| Annual budget | $1 million to $3 million |
| Staff size | 11 to 25 |
| Area of emphasis | Economic development |
| Years in operation | 11 to 25 |
| Geographic area | Western United States |

## Background

Sometimes even the best efforts can have unintended consequences. This NPO wanted community buy-in to their plan, so they conducted a series of "community visioning" events to gather input. One of the Key Benchmarks that resulted from these meetings was that the average private-sector earnings per job would exceed the U.S. average by the year 2000.

This goal sounded very possible, and was supported by the community. The thought was that the area must close the gap between its average earnings per job and the national average, which is a noble pursuit. The reality of the situation, though, was that this agreed-upon metric was virtually impossible to reach.

## Primary Use of ROI/OVP Material

- Build community consensus.
- Build support for investment.

## The ROI Framework

This situation was not normal in that the value of the NPO's efforts did not need to be quantified—it needed to be debunked. The challenge was to provide evidence that the metric put forth by the community was not realistic. Area values for existing jobs and earnings were used to illustrate the problem and provide guidance for more realistic goal setting.

## Value Proposition Presented

In trying to distill this "key benchmark" into a usable goal, objective data was gathered on which several scenarios could be developed. The inputs used are shown in Exhibit 10.8.

**Scenario 1: Creating 5,000 New Jobs at $35,000/yr**   As a starting point, 5,000 jobs/yr at $35,000/yr for five years were analyzed, as shown in Exhibit 10.9.

### EXHIBIT 10.8    OBJECTIVE INPUTS

| | |
|---|---|
| Goal supported by the community | 750 jobs/yr for 5 yrs = 3,750 total jobs |
| Local average earnings per job | $24,544 |
| U.S. average earnings per job | $28,291 |
| Local total earnings, place of work | $5,504,993,000 |
| Local total employment | 224,287 |
| Average earnings per job | $5,504,993,000/224,287 = $24,544 |

**EXHIBIT 10.9     THE IMPACT OF 5,000 JOBS AT $35,000**

| | |
|---|---|
| $5,504,993,000 | Existing area earnings |
| +857,000,000 | 25,000 jobs × $35,000/job |
| $6,379,993,000 | Total new earnings |
| 224,287 | Existing area employment |
| +25,000 | 5,000 new jobs/yr |
| 249,287 | Total expected employment |
| $6,379,993,000 | Total new earnings |
| ÷249,287 | Total expected employment |
| $25,593 | New average earnings per job |

The new average earnings per job of $25,593 is only 4.3 percent higher than before, and is far from reaching the U.S. average of $28,291. This is holding the U.S. average constant over five years, which is a large assumption. The problem not fully realized in setting this key benchmark is that both the numerator and the denominator are affected in the calculation of average earnings per job.

**Scenario 2: The $112,000 Job**   Working backwards, what would it take to reach the national average in earnings per job?

Exhibit 10.10 uses 2,000 jobs per year (for a total of 10,000).

**EXHIBIT 10.10     THE IMPACT OF 2,000 JOBS AT $112,000**

Solving for $x$

$$\frac{x}{(224,287 \text{ existing jobs} + 10,000 \text{ new jobs})} = \$28,291$$

$$x = \$6,628,213,000$$

| | |
|---|---|
| $6,628,213,000 | Total new earnings |
| ÷234,287 | Total expected employment |
| $28,291 | New average earnings per job |
| $6,628,213,000 | Total new earnings |
| −$5,504,993,000 | Current earnings |
| $1,123,220,000 | Earnings difference |
| $1,123,220,000 | Earnings difference |
| ÷10,000 | New jobs created |
| $112,322 | New average earnings per job |

These 10,000 new jobs, which is 2½ times the program goal, would have to pay an average of $112,322, which was unrealistic and over four times what the existing average job paid.

## Takeaway Message

While the goal of bringing the local economy up to national levels sounded good and was widely supported, it was unlikely to be realized. The NPO did not want to put itself in a position where it could not reach its goals. The importance of realistic goals was reinforced, and new goals were set that would allow the organization the chance to succeed.

# ORGANIZATION 8: MAKING THE ECONOMIC PIE BIGGER

## Profile

| | |
|---|---|
| Type of organization | 501 (c) (3) |
| Annual budget | $500,000 to $1 million |
| Staff size | 1 to 10 |
| Area of emphasis | Economic development |
| Years in operation | 11 to 25 |
| Geographic area | Eastern United States |

## Background

This economic development organization was faced with a not–uncommon situation: Why would existing employers want to invest in a program whose goal is to bring in more employers? Dominant employers in any community have screamed for years that new industry will drive up their own labor costs and cut into their profitability. Conventional wisdom tells us that this is correct. Unfortunately, conventional wisdom often disregards basic economics.

Finding themselves at the beginning of the launch of their new capital campaign, this NPO was faced with the fact that the largest employer in the area would not be an investor in the effort because they thought new industry would drive up their own labor costs. The labor situation in the area was tight, and they wanted no more competition to attract employees. Being the dominant employer, they carried both economic and political weight in the community. The organization needed an ROI-based case that would turn this employer around, or the campaign would be stalled before it even started.

### Primary Use of ROI/OVP Material

- Enlist leadership.

- Demonstrate value to the entire community.

### The ROI Framework

This task could only be accomplished by a watertight economic argument. What needed to be demonstrated was that the large employer's profitability would not be hurt by the efforts of the NPO and, in fact, their long-term profitability possibly could be improved. The example produced contained very few numbers, and relied on economic theory.

### Value Proposition Presented

The following economic logic was applied:

- The creation of new jobs, and the subsequent increase in population, property and sales taxes, and so on is *how economies grow.* The short-term rise in operating costs of an individual employer should be offset by an increase in the standard of living of the area *if* the jobs that are being created are higher quality jobs.

- If one believes in the theory that it is better (for a company and/or the local economy) to have a major employer in town without any labor competition, taking this premise to the extreme demonstrates its shortcomings. If it were indeed better for a business to be the only major player in town, wouldn't businesses be moving to smaller towns where this would be the case? Instead, the opposite happens, where growing businesses tend to locate in areas where there are other growing businesses, thereby increasing the labor pool.

- If a local economy is considered relatively better (all other things being equal) than some other place, people will naturally migrate there. The

EXHIBIT 10.11      **SUPPLY AND DEMAND OF LABOR**

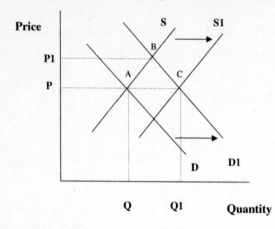

1. Price (wages) and quantity (labor) are at equilibrium at point A.
2. New companies come into town and force the demand for labor up to line D1, which
   causes wages to go up to P1, and the new equilibrium point shifts to B.
3. In response to increased wages, more qualified labor is attracted to town, which
   causes supply to increase to S1, and the new equilibrium shifts to C.
4. Point C is at the same wage level as when we started.

same holds true with individual companies. The fact that they are not migrating to the employer in question signifies that (1) they are not paying enough, (2) the local economy is not very good, or (3) it was a bad business decision by the company to locate in an area where the labor supply and wage rates do not meet their requirements.

- Forward thinking in economic development believes that clusters, not individual companies, drive an economy. Clusters can provide synergy, which can lead to competitive advantage. An emphasis on keeping an existing employer happy (in other words, artificially insulated from free market competition) will not drive an economy in the future.

- Diversification of industry can help the economy of an area only from an economic portfolio perspective.

- A number of employers demanding a more qualified workforce will naturally bring more influence to improve an educational and/or training system than a single employer will.

- What *may* be good for the employer in question in the short run will *probably* be bad for the local economy in the long run. What the employer is saying in economic terms is that the demand for labor has reached the level that any further increase in demand will put upward pressure on wages. This is a correct statement, but only half the story. Economically, an increase in demand will cause the price of anything to rise, but *the quantity supplied will also rise!* People will move to an area where good jobs are available.

- The economic argument is this: When there are increases in demand, both supply *and* demand shift, quantity will increase, and prices will likely stay the same. The display in Exhibit 10.11 demonstrates this.

## Takeaway Message

Economies sometimes work in strange ways, but not in this case. While in the short term, some upward pressure on wages may be felt, in the long run, the labor pool will be deeper and the local economy will be stronger. Then again, as John Maynard Keynes said, "In the long run, we are all dead."

# Index

Printed in the United States of America
ED-10-09-11